GARDENING

Image: Public Domain Pixabay

Hydroponics for Self Sufficiency-

Vegetables, Herbs & Berries

Melissa Honeydew

Melissa Honeydew

Table of Contents

Melissa Honeydew

Introduction

I want to thank you and congratulate you for buying the book, "Hydroponics for Beginners: The Ultimate Guide to Hydroponic Gardening".

This book contains a great deal of information on how to start, grow and provide your own food using the methods included in Hydroponic Gardening.

We will go over the entire process from selecting the right systems, using the right Nutrients and Mediums and answering questions that many beginners ask such as "What can I grow?" "How long does it take?" "Can I do this at my home?" and "How can I get started?"

Continuous cultivation of crops has caused the soil quantity around the world to decline that has resulted in lower yields as well as lowered quality of the crops. Moreover, conventional cropping techniques require a lot of space as well as labor, which with the passage of time is becoming harder to find at competitive rates. In the wake of these events, a new soil-less crop growing technique has been developed known as hydroponics. Hydroponics is a soil-less technique that offers a solution to counter all the aforementioned problems and which offers optimum opportunities for plants to grow, allowing a higher yield to be obtained in many cases.

Moreover, it can be carried out right in your own backyard. Want to know how? Read on!

Thanks again for buying this book, I hope you enjoy it and that it gives you all the information you need to get you enthused toward growing your own crops in this way.

Chapter 1

Getting to Know This System Better

Soil is the most common growing medium available in the world and therefore plants are normally grown in it because it's the established way of growing. It provides nutrients, air, water and anchorage that are some of the most vital factors required for proper plant growth. However, sometimes soil poses a serious limitation, e.g. in remote areas or areas which suffer drought and depend on the weather. Moreover, increased presence of disease and insecticide resistant pests have substantially raised the concern for growing plants at home.

Hydroponics is a soil-less technology that allows growing plants in nutrient solutions that contain all the elements and compounds necessary for the correct growth of plants. The technique has been around for some time now and has been in practice since ancient civilizations including the times of the Egyptians, Chinese, Babylonians and Amazons. The world rediscovered the technique almost a hundred years ago with the sudden boom of the greenhouse industry. Since then, the popularity of hydroponics gardening has been on the rise.

The reason for its success is simple. If a plant is given all the necessary nutrients it needs to grow, in the amount it needs, then undoubtedly the plant will grow as genetically healthy as possible. And surprisingly, this target is much more achievable through hydroponics compared to soil. With hydroponic techniques, the plant grows in a perfectly balanced inert growing medium with the pH adjusted to the right amount. Don't let these words scare you as all the answers to your questions will soon follow. The nutrient solution is then delivered to the roots in a very soluble form which allows the plants to absorb the nutrients quite easily compared to in soil where most of the roots are spread wide and deep and need to search for nourishment. This allows for faster and better growth of plants in a safe manner, which is why the revolution is gaining momentum.

Now for your questions, what is growing medium? Growing medium is basically the material in which the roots of a plant grow like soil or, in this case, alternate materials. In hydroponics, growing medium is not responsible for providing nutrition to the plants; instead it is the nutrient solution's duty to give the plants the nutrients they need. This allows the whole process to be controlled much more easily. The pH and other chemical properties of the solution are easier to adjust and can be optimized according to the plant's needs thus saving money. Moreover, the whole process can be controlled using a computer or a timer and requires very little human intervention.

What is pH? Right now, all you need to know about pH is that it is an extremely important factor in the whole process. Plants can lose the ability to absorb nutrients with variations in pH. The pH for most of the hydroponic crops must be maintained in between 5.5 and 6.5. However, ask your gardener or culture-provider for the exact requirements for a particular crop. Much the same as in soil the acidity and alkaline properties of nutrients are determined by the pH.

Coming to the fertilizers, both hydroponic and conventional fertilizers used in soil contain 3 major nutrients namely,

1. Nitrogen,

2. Phosphorus,

3. Potassium,

The only major difference between the two types of fertilizers is that hydroponics fertilizers contain the right ratio of the all the nutrients that plants require to be grown, which means the three shown above as well as trace elements like calcium, sulfur, magnesium and iron which soil already possesses. Also, organic fertilizers rely on bacterial action whereas hydroponic fertilizers pack everything in the right amount and in a ready-to-use format.

For the common man, hydroponics gardening may sound like a complex set of practices, but it doesn't have to be that way. If only you were to realize the benefits you would gain from the technique, you would never think of growing in any other way. It can be as simple as growing a single plant in a nursery pot and won't require any automation unless you plan to open a full-scale business based on hydroponics. The average home system would only include a growing tray, a reservoir, a pump and air stone so that the solution remains oxygenated. I'll instruct you on how to build your own system later on!

The name suggests that the system uses water as the base. Let us try to understand why it is that we use water as the base instead of any other solvent. Let us assume that there was no water on earth. Would you be able to survive? How would you quench your thirst? There are numerous probes and satellites that have been launched into deep space to discover planets that have water on them; what people have forgotten is that our planet is covered in water, literally three fourths of it!

Every cellular organism and majestic beast craves for water. It is only because of the existence of water that there are living beings on this planet! Well, this book is all about water! It is a lovely way to help you learn how you can manage the water resources in your surroundings and also combine that with certain nutrition in order to grow plants well in your backyard!

You will need to remember that water and fire always work together when it comes to providing the plants with nutrition. When there is a forest that has been burnt down, the wood from every single tree will turn to ash. This ash contains potassium – a mineral that is extremely important for the whole of the plant kingdom! When the monsoon arrives, the water helps in washing the leaves and the branches that have decayed over a few days. This process is hastened by the insects and other microorganisms. They also excrete organic waste once they have helped in the clearing of debris. This excreted organic waste is what the plants will feed on. The organic waste contains numerous minerals and vitamins that are needed by the plants.

When the monsoon brings in the rain, the water helps in diluting the organic waste. This diluted state makes it easy for the plants to absorb the minerals and vitamins they need to grow.

If you are looking for different ways to ensure that your plants have obtained a balance diet, you will need to ensure that there is perfect harmony between every element in nature. The forests have to burn, the insects and microorganisms must eat, and the monsoons must rush in, the wood needs to decay so that the microbes in the soil help the plants in the absorption of the nutrients required. You will never find such a situation anywhere except in a rainforest.

Hydroponics is a process where you work towards enriching the water with nutrients and salts that are always found in nature. You will need to create a solution that provides your plants with a balanced environment. You will come to realize over the course of the book that every hydroponic system always contains a solution that is abundant with nutrients. This system works towards protecting that solution from evaporating into the environment. This approach to manage water is why it is good to use hydroponics in areas that are barren and parched throughout the year. This system has gained popularity through the name 'Earth Friendly Gardening'.

You will be working with a form of art called water gardening. It is therefore wise to understand the contents of the water you will be using. You will need to contact the water company and understand and analyze every minute detail about the water. If you know that the water you use comes from a well, you will need to send it to the lab for an analysis. The factor that is of utmost importance is the hardness or softness of water. If the water is hard, this implies that the water contains a lot of minerals, especially calcium carbonate. If the water you use is soft, you will find that it is pure. If you have distilled water or have passed it through the process of reverse osmosis, it is considered to be soft water. There are numerous specifications for the nutrient solution you will need to use when it comes to hard or soft water. You will need to keep these points in mind when you are purchasing nutrients for the solution.

You have to remember that you are working with plants. The plants always absorb all the nutrients required through their roots. You have to make sure that you pay a great deal of attention to the roots. Make sure that you do not submerge the roots too much. You have to keep in mind that these roots need to have enough oxygen that is circulating in the water.

If you want the roots to be healthy, you have to make sure that the water circulates well throughout the reservoir. You have to make sure that there is no stagnation since that may lead to the death of all plants! The loveliest part of the hydroponics system is that you can always grow different types of plants without having to worry about the weather. You need to have the perfect nutrient solution and the perfect protection for your plants and you will have the best yield ever!

Chapter 2

A Quick Overview of Hydroponics

Hydroponics is a one of the wonders of modern science. You will find that the gardens that use hydroponics systems tend to have an abundance of fruits, flowers, vegetables, herbs, grains and many other types of food you probably would have never found before in your country. The system helps in producing crops that are extremely healthy and also have the highest yield. They have a good level of vitamin in their bodies due to the balanced nutrient solution!

The newer techniques of hydroponics help in providing the world with food that is superior to the same food that has been cultivated elsewhere. Since the cultivation of crops through hydroponics is extremely effective, NASA has chosen to cultivate crops in space in the similar way. It was when experiments were conducted to understand the chemical composition of plants that the science behind hydroponics came into existence. You will be surprised to know that these experiments date back to 1600 AD. There are records that state that plants were cultivated in mixtures of gravel and sand, without using soil, even in the older times. You will not believe that the hanging gardens of Babylon and the floating gardens of the Aztecs are in fact examples of hydroponic gardening in the older times. There are certain hieroglyphics in Egypt, which show that people had chosen to cultivate their plants in water alone!

It was in 1936 that the word hydroponics was coined by a scientist named Dr. W.F. Gericke. He had chosen this word in order to describe the combination of cultivating plants that are both ornamental and edible while using a solution with water and nutrients. The word literally translates to 'Hydro' meaning water and 'Ponos' meaning labor.

You have been told above that this method of gardening uses a nutrient solution to provide the plants with all that it needs in order to be healthy. The nutrient solution that is in this system circulates around the roots using the forces of gravity. There are certain hydroponic systems that use a pump that works on electricity. There are some systems that have an extremely simple way of working. They let the roots of the plants stay in the nutrient solution while using an air pump to ensure that the solution flows continuously. It is best to ensure that the solution continues to flow since stagnation will cause your system to fail.

You will find that the plants that you have grown using the hydroponics system are in fact stronger and healthier than the plants that have been grown conventionally. You will learn over time that this is true since the nutrient solution provides your plants with a balanced diet. The plants are also extremely safe from any form of pest. The efficient hydroponics systems are always great at conversing and managing the water in the system. The system also helps in ensuring that the water does not evaporate.

If you find that the area you live in is extremely dry, you will find that you can grow cops easily if you use the hydroponics systems. These systems always deliver the water and also provide all your plants with the nutrients that they desperately need. You will be able to grow all the crops together, which will help you conserve space too! When you grow your crops in a clean environment, and under conditions that are ideal, you will find yourself saving a lot of money. You do not have to spend any money on the soil or even spend any money on the chemicals you would need in order to ensure that your crops grow very well.

When you use the traditional methods of farming, you will find that there is a lot of energy that you will be able to save. You will find that the plants are less healthy when compared to the plants that have been cultivated through hydroponics systems. You will find that the plants have been given all the minerals they need and will be able to produce more flowers, vegetables and fruits!

The plants that have been grown hydroponically are always healthier. You will find that they receive the balanced diet that they desperately need. The plants have a lot of energy and are strong in any type of weather. These plants are tastier and more nutritious as well. The next chapter helps you understand the system of hydroponics better!

Understanding the nutrient solution

Let us try to understand the strength of a plant first. You can compare the strength of the plant to that of a chain. You may have heard the proverb 'A chain is as strong as its weakest link'.

You have to always ensure that your chain is strong. You need to ensure that every link is in place and has a good supply. You have to ensure the right nutrients have been added to the solution. Make sure that the solution is concentrated since the plants are dependent on these nutrients. But, you have to learn that each plant has its own separate requirements when it comes to nutrients.

The nutrients that are available commercially always come with instructions that will help you understand the proportions you will need to mix. You will also learn what type of solution you will need to provide a plant with at different stages of germination. There are numerous products that are available commercially in the market. This is why it is easy to make your way through hydroponics. You will not find it difficult even if you are a beginner since you do not have to make your own nutrients for your plants.

When you choose a nutrient to work with, there are certain things you will need to watch out for. The most important one is that the nutrient needs to be designed to be used for the hydroponic application alone! You should never try to use any supplements for the same. This is for the reason that the medium you are using to grow your crops does not have microorganisms that help in the transfer of the nutrients from these supplements into the plants. You can use powders that have multi purposes. But, only use them when the lighting conditions are poor.

If you have decided to go ahead and grow your plants in direct sunlight, you will need to use a powder, which has two different functions. This will increase the yield of the plants that finally grow. There is an extremely simple reason behind this. The first is that the multipurpose nutrients help in satisfying different ranges of plants and will also help the plant grow in different conditions. You will find that you cannot bend the uses of these powders for one particular plant. The other reason is that you can blend these powders in two or three different liquids forming two or three different solutions, which could be administered to the plant at different stages of growth. An extremely powerful technique is the one where you learn to optimize the growth of your garden through this method.

There are a few people out there who may choose to prepare their own nutrients. There are a few recipes that have been given below. These will help you prepare your nutrients for your plants. You can use these nutrients at different stages of growth for the plant!

Recipes for Nutrients

If you are someone who loves creating your very own nutrients, you will find this chapter interesting. If you are someone who loves chemistry, you will love this chapter!

Vegetative Nutrient

Amount: 5 liters

Nitrogen: 19

Phosphorous: 12

Potassium: 24

Ingredients

0.43 oz Calcium Nitrate

1.6 oz Potassium Nitrate

2.2 oz Sulfate of Potash

0.1 oz Monopotassium Phosphate

1.8 oz Magnesium Sulfate

0.7 oz Fe Chelated Trace Elements

Instructions

You will need to mix these ingredients well together and add five liters of water in order to form the nutrient solution.

Fruiting Nutrient

Amount: 5 liters

Nitrogen: 16

Phosphorous: 11

Potassium: 25

Ingredients

5.6 oz Calcium Nitrate

1.6 oz Potassium Nitrate

1.4 oz Sulfate of Potash

1.1 oz Monopotassium Phosphate

2.1 oz Magnesium Sulfate

0.7 oz Fe Chelated Trace Elements

Instructions

You will need to mix these ingredients well together and add five liters of water in order to form the nutrient solution.

Flowering Nutrient

Amount: 5 liters

Nitrogen: 11

Phosphorous: 16

Potassium: 37

Ingredients

3.5 oz Calcium Nitrate

1.8 oz Potassium Nitrate

0.7 oz Sulfate of Potash

14 oz Monopotassium Phosphate

1.8 oz Magnesium Sulfate

0.4 oz Fe Chelated Trace Elements

Instructions

You will need to mix these ingredients well together and add five liters of water in order to form the nutrient solution.

Understanding the Chelated Trace Elements

These elements have a certain composition of their own. You will need to understand this combination first if you are willing to make your own nutrients. You have to make sure that this is the composition in order to ensure that you do not overdose the plant thereby harming it!

1. Iron – 7%

2. Manganese – 2%

3. Zinc – 0.4%

4. Copper – 0.1%

5. Boron – 1.30%

6. Molybdenum – 0.06%

Certain instructions to follow

If you are going to make your own nutrients there are certain rules you definitely need to follow. This section covers those rules.

You have to first fill the reservoir with clean and hot water. Make sure you fill three fourths of the reservoir. You will then have to multiply the quantities of each of the chemicals mentioned above with the gallons that your reservoir could hold. You will then need to add the chemicals one at a time in order to ensure that each salt has dissolved completely.

You have to remember that the salts used here are often active and reactive in their native states. When you are handling them make sure that you protect your eyes and your hands. You will need to follow all the instructions that have been given by the manufacturer.

How do you test the pH of the nutrient solution?

If you want to measure the pH of the nutrients in the solution, you will need to perform the measurement of PPM or TDS (Parts per million and Total dissolved solids respectively). You may have come across the term Electrical conductivity that is the exact same thing! This is because of the fact that you are measuring the electrical conductivity of the solution you have made.

There are a million ways to measure the PPM of a solution. The easiest one is by using the digital PPM gauge. You will need to submerge this in the solution and let the reading be taken. The lucky thing is that you do not have to work on calibration. If you keep changing the nutrient solutions, you will find that the concentrations are generally where they always need to be. It is always good to follow the directions that have been given for a particular nutrient. Try to replace the solution once in two weeks in order to obtain the best results.

Every nutrient in the world is useless to a plant if the plant cannot absorb that nutrient easily. For you to determine the ability of a plant to absorb the nutrients, you will need to understand the pH of the solution. The pH is always measured on a scale of 1 – 14. This represents the presence of the hydrogen ions in the solution. It is often used to determine the nature of a solution – acidic or basic. If there is a one on the scale, it implies that the concentration of the ion in the solution is low whereas the solution is neutral if the scale shows 7. If the scale shows 14, this implies that the solution is basic or alkaline. There are some nutrients that often become unavailable to the plants when the pH begins to drift from an optimal reading. You can test the pH simply using a litmus paper. You can do it the way you would have done it in chemistry class in school!

Chapter 3

What Can I Grow?

Hydroponics gardening techniques can be used to grow almost anything including flowering plants, houseplants, fruits and vegetables along with different types of herbs. Gardening indoors can provide you with a yearlong supply of fresh fruits and vegetables no matter what the season is. The choices are endless but I've made a list of the plants you can grow so that you have all the information that you need.

Vegetables

Many people who dwell in remote areas find it very hard to grow vegetables in their backyard. This is worse if they have no yard at all. Hydroponics gardening comes into the picture and, by using the technique; you'll be able to grow almost all vegetables in a much shorter time span.

When growing vegetable plants, be sure to plant them at least a foot apart so that the roots of vegetables don't mingle with each other. Among the vegetables that are optimum for growing hydroponically, these top the list:

Artichokes	Beets	Cabbages	Celery
Leeks	Parsnips	Radishes	Tomatoes
Asparagus	Broccoli	Carrots	Lettuce
Cucumber	Peas	Rhubarb	Yams
Beans	Brussel Sprouts	Eggplants	Cauliflowers
Onions	Potatoes	Squash	

However, the basic requirements for growing these vegetables remain the same as when grown in soil; you still have to provide these plants with appropriate sunlight, nutrition and pH control. You will have the advantage of growing all these foods all year round as indoor systems are becoming increasingly popular.

Fruits and Melons

Hydroponics will allow you to plant fruits and melons throughout the year irrespective of the weather conditions outside but you'll have to provide the crop with extra care and protect it against external enemies like pesticides and insects. Water loving fruits are a great choice for this technique and you'll be able to achieve quite a lot of success with the following fruits:

- Watermelon,

- Tomatoes,

- Cantaloupe,

- Blueberries,

- Strawberries,

- Blackberries,

- Grapes,

- Even pineapples.

Moreover, did you know that people have been successful in growing whole trees using hydroponics systems? That's right, trees like banana trees and dwarf citrus trees, i.e. lemon, etc. have been effectively grown using the techniques introduced by hydroponics gardening.

Herbs

Fresh herbs have been extremely popular throughout history and can be fun to grow too. Herbs have the ability to mature quite rapidly compared to other vegetables and a small hydroponic unit can give an impressive yield. You can grow the following herbs using the technique:

Arugula	Chives	Lemon balm	Oregano
Spear peppermint	Thyme	Basil	Coriander
Mache	Rosemary	Sage	Chervil
Dill	Marjoram	Sorrel	Tarragon

That's not it for hydroponic crops. There are a number of other crops as well which can be grown using this method but, unless you're a professional or have a lot of spare time, it's best to restrict yourself to the above plants as these respond well and easily to hydroponic methods.

Next, you'll learn about the different types of hydroponic systems.

Chapter 4

Types of Hydroponic Systems

There are a number of types of hydroponic systems but all of them have been derived from some kind of variation of 6 basic categories. These include:

Wick system

This particular system provides the simplest type of hydroponic units; being a passive system, i.e. no moving parts. The nutrient solution is drawn into the medium from a reservoir made up of a wick. The system is highly compatible and can use a wide variety of mediums, e.g. perlite, pro-mix, vermiculite and coconut fiber being the most common. The biggest drawback of this system is that plants that require a huge supply of water will use up the nutrient pool at a much faster rate than the wick is able to handle.

Water culture

Water culture based hydroponic systems use Styrofoam made platforms to hold the plants, which then float directly over the nutrient solution. An air pump is used to supply oxygen to the nutrient solution that is then provided to the roots. The system is used mostly for growing leafy vegetables and other water loving plants. Mostly lettuce is grown in this type of system due to their affinity to water. In addition, the system is popular in classrooms and is extensively used to teach children about hydroponic gardening. But the system does fall short when it comes to large or long-term plants.

Ebb and flow

The Ebb and flow unit works by flooding the grow tray with the nutrient solution for a short period of time and then draining it. This action is usually automated and set off by a timer connected to a submerged pump. When the timer turns the connected pump on, the solution is pumped from the reservoir to the tray and the opposite happens when the timer shuts down. The timer is usually set at many intervals during a day depending on the type of plants and the condition they are in.

With that being said, the Ebb and flow system is a versatile one and can be used with several growing mediums like grow rocks, granular Rockwool or gravel. You may use individual pots filled with these mediums if you want to increase the mobility of the plants, in and out of the system. The only major disadvantage of the system, due to the growing mediums, is vulnerability to power failure. The roots can dry out if the solution is not released at appropriate timings that can damage the yield. The problem can be rectified using a backup power source but that would only add cost to the whole unit.

Drip systems

One of the most widely used hydroponic gardening techniques in the world, drip systems are controlled through a submersed pump connected to a timer. The timer is used to turn on the pump that starts the dripping process, i.e. the nutrient solution starts dripping over each plant line. Furthermore, the excess nutrient can also be collected and reused as part of the reservoir.

In order to achieve this feat, the drip system must be recovery based otherwise the solution can't be recycled.

Recovery systems also add more efficiency to the whole process so even though you would have to make a higher investment in the beginning, the technique will eventually pay off.

On the other hand, a non-recovery technique would require a precise timer so that the least amount of nutrient solution is wasted. With that being said, the non-recovery system would require less maintenance compared to its recovery counterpart. Moreover, with this system, you won't need to worry about the pH of the solution since any used nutrients won't be recycled.

Nutrient Film Technique:

NFT systems have a continuous flow of nutrient solution so no timer is required in these types of units. The submersible pump, however, is still required to pump the nutrient into the growing tray and flows over the roots. The growing medium used for this system is usually air that brings down the cost of the whole system; normally the support mechanism used for the plants is a small plastic basket while the roots dangle in the nutrient solution.

Aeroponic

I saved the most technologically savvy system for last. Like the NFT system explained above, the Aeroponic system also uses air as a growing medium. Similarly, roots hang in the air and are soaked up in nutrient solution from time to time. In this case, a timer controls the pump and runs after a few minutes for a couple of seconds to keep the roots hydrated otherwise the yield will be affected.

Melissa Honeydew

Chapter 5

Pest Control

As you start growing your own plants using a hydroponic system you'll realize that your unit isn't entirely pest free so in order to take proactive measures against pests, natural products like pepper, tomato and garlic are used. They have certain advantages and these are the reasons they have been chosen:

- They are non-pollutants,

- No special equipment is required for their installation,

- They can be made easily,

- They are cheap,

- Unlike artificial pesticides, pests can't develop resistance to them.

Pepper

- Grind almost 3 ounces of pepper and add water to it.

- Let it stay for a night, then strain & mix with 5 liters of soap water.

- Apply on the plan on daily basis.

- Controls: worms, fleas, ants, chewers & flies

Garlic

- Mix 3 ounces of garlic with oil.

- Let it stand for a day.

- Dissolve 10 3.5 oz of soap in 1 liter of water; add 20 liters of water and mix.

- Mix both the solutions.

- Can be used as a repellant, fungicide and bactericide.

Tomato

- Grid the leaves and stems of a tomato.

- Boil them in 4 bottles of water for almost 10 minutes.

- Let the solution cool and then apply.

- Controls: lice, hairy worm and fleas.

Chapter 6

Growing Medium

As stated time and time again, a proper growing medium or substrate is necessary for a good yield. It may be solid or liquid but should pack a few of the following characteristics to say the least:

- It should consist of particles that are no smaller than 2 mm and no larger than 7 mm.

- It must not decompose easily,

- It should be capable of draining out excess liquid while maintaining the moisture content of the plant.

- It must be portable,

- It should be readily available,

- It should not hold off microorganisms toxic to humans,

- It should also not be contaminated with industrial waste,

The following is a list of recommended substrates:

- 50 percent rice hull: 50 percent ground volcanic stones,

- 60 percent rice hull: 40 percent ground clay bricks,

- 60 percent rice hull: 40 percent sand,

- 80 percent rice hill: 20 percent saw dust,

- Clean river water,

When working with rice hulls, make sure that they are washed and kept wet for 10 days so that all seeds germinate; these seeds should then be removed.

Sawdust, on the other hand, should be used with caution and more than 20 percent can prove harmful to plants.

Melissa Honeydew

Chapter 7

Bucket Bubbler System

This is one of the simplest hydroponic systems ever developed and that is exactly why I would like to start teaching you how to build your own unit from here. The system is much like a Water Culture system and the roots are suspended in nutrient. The system will make use of fertilizers and additives to give the plant all the nutrients that it needs.

The system that I'm about to teach you is designed for a single plant.

Material required

- 5 gallon bucket and lid – try to get a black colored gallon bucket or spray paint a transparent one if you can.

- Air pump, tubing and stone – these components will be required to oxygenate the solution. An air pump that fits into aquariums would work just as well.

- Netted cap – either purchase netted caps or make your own out of cups; the size of the raft will ultimately decide the number of cups and plants your system will have.

- Growing medium – a nominal amount of medium will be required, enough for a plastic cup to fit into.

- Water and nutrient mix.

Tools needed:

- Power drill – to cut holes in the lid,

- Hole saw – to adjust the size of netted pots,

- Drill bit – needed to drill ½" holes for water gauge and ¼" holes for air tubing,

- Tape measure – for the measurement of tubing sizes,

- Safety glasses,

- Knife – in case you don't have a drill

Assembly

1. First, drill a hole in the lid so that the plastic cups fit into it. Make sure that the cups you choose are durable and have tapered sides. Make the hole large enough so that the cup fits through the hole in the lid while, at the same time, the cup stays firm and does not fall through.

2. Drill a ¼" hole in the lid so that the air tube can fit into it perfectly.

3. Then, run the airline through the hole all the way down to the bottom of the bucket. Attach the air stone and leave enough airlines inside the bucket so that the stone lies flat on the bottom.

4. Fill the bucket with nutrient solution that has been prepared according to the fruit/vegetable's specific guidelines, just so it touches the netted cup. You may fill the bucket to a higher level if you want to sprout a seed.

5. Place the lid on the bucket.

6. After the roots grow a few inches below the cup, lower the level of the nutrient solution by an inch below the bottom surface of the cup.

7. Hook up the other end of the air-tube to an air pump and make sure that the nutrient water bubbles.

8. Once the bubbles appear, place your plant in the netted cup while its roots swirl from the bottom of the cup and fill it with the medium which may be either gravel or clay pellets.

9. Once the plant has been successfully planted into the growing medium, place the cup into the bucket's lid.

10. That's it!

System modifications

The system can be modified quite easily. You can add a water level gauge by cutting a ½" hole on the side of the bucket and insert a ½" rubber grommet. Connect this grommet to a ½" elbow and install a small piece of vinyl tubing that is directed to the top of the bucket.

The systems may also be linked with a central reservoir using ½" rubber grommets, 1/2" vinyl tubing and ½" barbed fittings.

In addition, the system can be recreated using a number of different materials that can hold water and are dark in color.

One material in particular that is gaining a lot of popularity is Rubbermaid ® totes which allow much more space to hold the plants.

Care instructions

Keep on monitoring the water level in the system and make sure that it does not get too low so that the plant suffers. Add more water once the plants utilize all the nutrient rich water and recheck the pH, adjusting it accordingly. Don't add excessive fertilizer unless advised otherwise or your solution will become bogged down and harmful to the plants.

Change the nutrient solution by draining it once the plants use the nutrient solution for the second time.

Melissa Honeydew

Chapter 8

Ebb and Flow System

The Ebb and Flow system as described in Chapter 3 is known for its easy build and maintenance, flexible design and automation. Plants that have been placed individually in pots are placed on a growing bed that holds a known amount of water. From time to time, the timer activates the pumping mechanism and the nutrient solution is pumped into the grow bed from the reservoir. The plants are watered from the bottom through the drain holes and after the plants have been watered for a couple of seconds, the pump turns off; usually the flood and drain cycle repeats 2 – 4 times a day. The system as a whole is very versatile, affordable and reliable and can easily handle 4, 6 inch pots. Here's how you can make one by using the materials available at the hardware store.

Material required

- Rubbermaid Black Storage Tote w/ Lid – 16 to 20 gallons,
- Rubbermaid Snap-toppers Clear Tote – 28 to 34 quart,
- Electric timer – 15 minute increments,
- Air pump, air stone and air tubing,
- Netted pots,
- Black irrigation tubing,
- Water pump,
- Growing medium – clay or any other cheap medium like gravel,
- Fill and drain,
- Water & nutrient mix.

Tools needed

- Power drill – to cut holes in the lid,

- Hole saw – 1 to ¼" holes,

- Drill bit – needed to drill ½" holes for water gauge and ¼" holes for air tubing,

- Tape measure – for the measurement of tubing sizes,

- Teflon tape – for sealing bulkheads,

- Safety glasses,

- Knife – in case you don't have a drill machine

Assembly

1. Start out by cutting 2, 1 – ¼" holes in the center of the topper tray; smooth out the rough edges by rubbing them against sandpaper. Remember that your pots must fit around these holes so always have a rough estimate in your mind about the width of the drain holes.

2. After successfully cutting the drain holes, place the tray on the top of the tote lid and center it. Mark the center of each hole going through the tray and onto the lid using a marker. Cut the two 1 – ¼" holes into the lid right where you marked them; the basic idea is to line the holes so that the drain fittings superimpose properly.

3. Cut out 2 additional 1 – ¼" holes into both of the sides of the top of the lid, one being for pump plug while the other being to measure the nutrient level and add more solution as the level falls.

4. Now, screw the drain fittings into the holes located in the clear container only. The rubber gasket must go on the underside of the bin so tighten the screws using your hand; using tools will only increase the risk of stripping these fittings out.

5. Place the ½" irrigation tubing over the pump's outlet fitting. The type of hosing you use would have a direct impact over the securing mechanism; you may need to use a zip tie for this purpose.

6. Place the container with drain fittings in line with the holes on the lid so that all these parts line up perfectly and snap down onto the lid.

7. Cut the 1/2" tubing to a length that allows the pump to lay down on the bottom of the reservoir when the lid is on. Push the tubing over the port of the ½" inflow tube from the bottom of the lid and use a zip tie to tightly harness it.

8. Place the air stone at the bottom of the reservoir and run the tubing through the side access hole. Lace the lid on top of the tote and snap it shut.

9. Use a piece of wood to make a dipstick and as you pour 5 liters of water into the reservoir, submerge part of the dipstick and mark the levels at each point of the dipstick until it completely submerges. This will help you keep track of the nutrient water level without having to remove the plants, tray or lid.

10. Add in 10 gallons of water to the reservoir and add a nutrient concentrate of your choice. Once added, check the pH of the solution and adjust it if needed. Then, plug in the water and air pump to diagnose the system of any error and if no leaks are found then take the next step.

11. Take the pots and drill several ¼" holes around their sides and in their bottoms to allow proper drainage of nutrient solution. Now fill each of the pots with growing medium of your choice, e.g. clay balls.

12. Plant your vegetables, fruits or flowers into the pits and pack the medium around the plant carefully so that the roots are not damaged. It is best to start off with pellets and then plant them into the pots so that nutrient solution can keep the plant moist all the way to the top.

When planting seeds, be sure to keep watering the plants for the first few weeks.

System modifications

This particular system allows easy scaling and can be converted into a small-scale business quite easily, the only limiting factors being the size of the tray and the subsequent amount of plants that can fit into it.

Care and Feeding

As soon as your plants consume half of the nutrient solution, add more water to bring the level back up. Recheck and adjust the pH value but add no fertilizer yet. When the plants utilize the nutrient solution for the second time, drain the existing solution from the reservoir and make up a new batch of nutrient solution. Pour this into the reservoir.

Chapter 9

NFT System

NFT or Nutrient Film Technique Systems are one of the most widely used hydroponics as well as aquaponics template when it comes to growing plants on a bigger scale. The Nutrient Film Technique makes use of a tube to hold the plants still and provides them with nutrient infused water that stays in constant contact with the roots of the plants. The technique is quite flexible and allows a person to grow plants ranging from lettuce to tomatoes. In addition, the system can be modified in a number of ways and the possibilities are seemingly endless in terms of size, materials and layouts.

The roots of the plant are grown in sealed, shallow and light-resistant channel while the nutrient solution is swirled constantly over the roots, almost 24 hours every day. The technique was even named because of the nature of the system as it requires the liquid to flow past the roots at a shallow depth so that the plants get enough oxygen.

The NFT system uses no growing media that means that holding the moisture can sometime become a problem and plants can dry out soon. To rectify this issue, the system uses frequent watering cycles and some growers even leave the water open all day, but in the end that's up to you to decide. For starters, you can set the timer or water manually after every half an hour until a perfect point is found. The nutrient reservoir in an NFT system is built with at least 2 channels that allow water to circulate around the system. The reservoir is must within any hydroponics system as water needs to stored & drawn from it so that the pump does not burn up.

In addition to using water pump for circulating water throughout the system, this technique also uses the natural force of gravity to assist in this entire process. Each of the ends of the

PVC are placed higher than the subsequent one so that water enters the highest and is drawn downwards automatically though gravitational potential energy. These downward supports can be built out of a variety of material that include lumber, PVC, etc. You can also hang them from a stationary support so that the water returns back to it.

Supplies

- 4 inch PVC pipes of 10 inch lengths, cut into 3 portions,

- A 2 x 6 inch NFT stand or a 2 x 4 frame,

- 1 – 1 ½ inch wooden screws,

- 4 inch rubber end caps along with hose clamps,

- 1 x submersible pump,

- Air pumps, tubing & stones,

- 3 inch netted cups,

- ½ inch – ¾ inch irrigation tubing,

- Rubber grommets,

- 4 straight connectors,

- 5 gallon bucket or container or aquaponics fish tank,

- Hydroponic nutrient,

Tools

- Saw,
- Drill,
- Utility knife,
- 3 inch hole saw,
- Standard screwdriver,
- Screws

Assembly

1. After deciding on the type of container you will be using for your reservoir, start designing your stands. The first thing to keep in mind while doing so is to design them in such a way that they are taller than the reservoir. For this example system, you may use stand heights ranging from 14 inch to 19 inch.

2. Cut lengths out of the 2 x6 stand, cut a triangle out of each of the lengths so that the PVC can be held at one place. Next, join them together with the 2 x 4s by placing the 2 x 4s horizontally.

3. Next, drill a hole for the tubing so that it connects into each of the caps using a spade bit. Drill these holes at the heights where you want the water level to stay. Also, keep in mind that the holes should be high enough so that the

water level is enough to submerge the bottom of each cup. You can also make it adjustable by placing a hole on the outer side of the fitting and adjust the water height by rotating the rubber fitting.

4. When purchasing the pump, make sure that it comes with a removable attachment that can be bound to a piece of tubing in case you need to reach the upper part of the tube from the bottom of the reservoir.

5. Now push the tube that is joined to the NFT fitting through the hole. Take another piece of tubing with NFT fitting long enough to reach the upper side of the tube. Repeat the same process from the lower tube to the reservoir/tank. Finally attach two end caps so that they fit on both the pieces of PVC.

6. The system will run well but if there are leaks then you may use plumbing cement to seal the outside of all the tubes. Toxicity wise, plumbing cement isn't the safest but using it only on the outside will keep your system free from any contamination. The substance will cure within 2 hours so another leak test can be performed fairly quickly.

7. If you are one of those people who like to clean everything with a bleach solution before using it then do

it before drilling any holes to maximize flow within the tubes; also shake the ends with the caps on.

8. Next, it's time to drill holes within the system that will depend on the type and size of the plants. The optimum number of plants is 6, which will require almost 8 – 9 inches of spacing between each hole. A hole saw would be your best bet when drilling these holes into the netted cups; use a 3-inch saw. You may use a dremel to cut out plastic from the cup but when doing so remember to be in a well-ventilated area and wearing a mask. Rinse the dust off the pipes after cutting them.

9. Drill 3 holes in the reservoir lid, each one serving its own specific purpose. Use 1 hole for the water supply line, one for the drain and the last one for power cord & air tubing.

10. Leave the lid on the container to help reduce the rate of evaporation as well as to provide protection against any debris that may fall into the container.

11. You can either use homemade netted pots or buy those available in hardware stores. If you buy them then they will be ready to use, otherwise you'll have to drill plenty of holes into the bottom and edges of each of the cup so that the roots of the plants can come in contact with the nutrient water.

12. The lower tubing should be directed to the side that faces the source of light that may be sun or an artificial light. Double check the stands and make sure that they are in the right orientation so that the water, when pumped at the highest point will slowly progress downwards without splashing or going out of the system.

13. After you find a growing medium, be sure that it is clean as well as sterilized before using it otherwise you may contaminate or worse infest your system with a host of insects & parasites. If you're purchasing medium from a store then all you need to do is rinse any dust or debris. In case of rock or gravel, you may wash it with Hydrogen peroxide. Also, be sure that the pH of the medium is close to neutral (7).

14. If you are transplanting the plant from soil then wash out as must dirt as you can because the dirt can become a source of blockage for the pump and clog it. Do not clean the plant too roughly as it could die and once the roots are clean, hold them in place with one hand while using the other to fill the netted pot with growing medium, concentrating around the roots.

When placing the plants in the system, place the taller ones at the back and the shorter ones out front so that sunlight is evenly distributed.

There are a total of 4 factors that have an influence over how the NFT system works:

1. Number of plants,

2. Size of channel tubing,

3. Capability of the pump,

4. Specs of the channel,

It's best to use a pump that isn't too small otherwise draining the solution would become a problem from time to time and there will also be a risk of early failure for the motor. The system can be transformed in a variety of ways and you're free to experiment with it to get the best out of it. This particular chapter gave you an example of the NFT system but modifications are seemingly endless, e.g. you may cut out each tube and make them of equal height so that they are fed as well as drained equally.

Chapter 10

Hydroponics Window Garden

Not everyone has the luxury of a backyard or a garden; many people are confined to cram up apartments and they have little room for any hydroponic activity. For these people, hydroponic window gardens are an ultimate choice that allows a person to make use of his/her windows and integrate it within a hydroponic system. The system works well for people who have limited access to sunlight. Water is pumped from the bottom of the container, made out of PVC piping to the upper reservoir that is responsible for guiding the water through a series of bottles that hold netted pots within them.

The netted pots that are fitted within the bottles hold the growing medium in which the plants are placed. The large bottles used within the system act as channeling mechanisms so that the earth's gravitational pull can be utilized and water can be directed downwards without any external energy consuming mechanism.

The 2 reservoirs and the entire garden are held still with the help of hooks, which are attached to a ceiling or another frame.

A variety of supplies is required for building such a system. These include:

- Water pump – inline or non-submersible pump will be optimum while the size will be dependent on the size of the head,

- Flexible irrigation tubing – 0.5 to 0.75 inches depending on the system's size,

- Irrigation connectors – the same ones used in NFT system,

- Netted pots – 2 to 3 inch diameter ones while the quantity depends on the size,

- Plastic bottles – depends on your requirement,

- Hooks,

- Ropes,

- Electric timer,

- Top reservoir,

- Rubber PVC caps,

- Bottom reservoir,

- Growing medium,

- 10 – 20 pounds of strong fishing line,

Remember that the reservoir, both top & bottom should be waterproof and made of PVC or any other plastic material.

Tools

- Scissors,

- Utility knife,

- Drill bits,

- Drill,

Assembly

1. Select the window that you'll be using for the hydroponics system. Once selected, take the length, breadth and height of the window as well as its surrounding areas so that you'll be prepared to make adjustments to your system in case you need to. This step in particular is quite essential; otherwise you might end up making a system that does not fit within the selected window!

2. Choose the type of reservoir that you'll be using, i.e. will it be hanging from the roof or sitting on a floor? After choosing this, determine the height from where the pump will have to work to get the water. This height will be called the "head height" and will be helpful when you go to the market to purchase a pump.

3. By now you would have the pump size, the design of the system as well as the placement of reservoir in place. Take the width of the window into account and cut some 3 inch PVC to the same size as the window. If you are making use of the bottom reservoir, then cut 2 pieces.

4. After cutting these holes, cut another hold in the top of the bottom reservoir. This hole will act as a drainage hole where the plastic bottle will drain.

5. Drill a hole into one of the caps used in the bottom reservoir that will allow the straight slip NFT connector to get through and supply water to the pump.

6. Take the plastic containers and cut hole into the bottom of one of these; the hole must be 1 inch in diameter.

7. Once again use the plastic bottles or containers and cut a single hole in one of their sides. Make an oval cut 3 quarters from the top.

8. Make 2 holes in the top of the plastic bottles from where the fishing line will enter through one end and leave through another. The string will run through each of the bottles and will tie them up to the top of the reservoir.

9. Now, install the top & bottom reservoirs by connecting the additional plumbing lines to the pump, through the

reservoir. Once connected, take the plastic bottles and tie them to the upper reservoir so that they stand straight.

10. Finally, the moment you've been waiting for: planting the plant! Fill the netted pots with a handful of growing medium (the lighter the better) and plant your fruit/vegetable root into it.

11. Place the netted cups into the holes that were cut earlier in the plastic containers. If the bottles don't fit properly then expand the holes and tip the cups at a certain angle. Tie another piece of string to the plastic bottle's neck so that it doesn't fall off.

12. Test the system by filling it up with the nutrient solution. Make sure that there are no leaks and if any errors surface, rectify them immediately.

Hydroponic Window Gardens can be altered in a number of ways quite easily using various materials. However, there are 3 factors that play a major role in such modifications and should always be on your mind:

1. The size of the plants,

2. The size of the water pump,

3. The size of the bottles,

The tubing size and the pump size should be compatible; otherwise the reservoir will flood too frequently.

Chapter 11

Floating Hydroponic Garden

When the Spanish conquistadors invaded South America, they were quite impressed by the Aztecs' floating gardens. Now, it's the 21st century and you can still amaze your neighbors with your very own hydroponic garden for under 50$ and there's the added benefit of fresh fruits & vegetables which I almost forgot to mention!

Construction steps

- Using a 2 x 6 inch or 2 x 8 inch piece of treated lumber, make a rectangular frame that is 1 inch long, 1 inch wide by 8 feet and 4 feet high. The size of the frame negates the need for trimming the Styrofoam that floats in the solution. You may change the size of the frame if you are already familiar with the whole process.

- Line the entire frame with a 6-ml plastic sheet so a trough is formed that will contain the nutrient solution. Make sure that the site is leveled and free of any debris so that any potential puncture incident can be avoided.

- Secure one of the ends of the plastic liner to the top edge of the frame with 1x2 inch strips or lattice using either screws or nails.

- Place a 4x8 foot, 1 ½ inch thick Styrofoam sheet within the lined frame, making sure that edges have enough room to allow the garden vertical movement. If you want, adjust the frame so that the Styrofoam superimposes over it.

- Fill the garden with almost 20 gallons of water so that it forms a plastic sheeting to the sides of the frame.

- Secure the other end of the plastic liner with the top edge of the frame.

- Keep on filling the garden until the water reaches a height of 5 inches; record the amount of water you're pouring by noting down the number of gallons you've added.

- Add fertilizer that is soluble in water, i.e. 20 x 20 x 20 or 24 x 8 x 16 and remember to add micronutrients as well. Add 1 – 2 level teaspoons for each gallon of water you add to the garden. Moreover, add Magnesium sulfate at a steady rate of ½ to 1 level teaspoon for every gallon of water. Use a soft broom to mix both the ingredients thoroughly before adding to the water garden.

- The pH of the final solution must lie in between 5.5 and 6.5 If not, then add vinegar to bring down the pH.

- Light showers will have little effect on the garden and only heavy flooding will disturb the balance of micronutrients. You'll need to add more micronutrients after that. The same procedure must be followed and therefore you must keep track of the number of gallons of water that flooded the hydroponic garden.

- You can grow two crops of green vegetables before the nutrient solution must be changed.

- Use a sharp knife to cut holes in Styrofoam; a 2 ½ inch saw would be needed to drill down the correct sized holes into the Styrofoam. The size of the hole should allow a 3" net pot to level with the lower side of the Styrofoam; adjust the thickness according the depth of the Styrofoam. It is vital that you check the extension of each cup and make sure that it is not lower than 1/16 inches below the surface of the Styrofoam sheet. If this happens then your plant will be at the risk of dying.

- Keep the optimum plant spacing in mind, i.e. 6 inches from the side, 12 inches apart; this will allow 32 holes to be planted.

- Place the young starter transplants directly into the cups and use pointy tools like toothpicks to hold the plant in a 90 degree position. Neither should you pack any additional media nor should you remove the soilless media from the spaces around the plant; the transplant root ball should sit inside the cup, surrounded by air.

- After placing the transplant in the net pot or Styrofoam cup, add extra water and fertilizer to the container so that the sheet keeps on floating in the solution.

Crops

The floating hydroponic gardens can be used to cultivate the following crops:

1. Lettuce,

2. Mustard greens,

3. Mint,

4. Chives,

5. Kale,

6. Basil,

7. Cucumber,

8. Swiss chard,

9. Watercress,

10. Sunflowers.

Melissa Honeydew

Chapter 12

Hydroponic Cucumbers

Hydroponic Cucumbers are one of the most popular produce of hydroponics systems and can be grown in a variety of ways. This method in particular involves the use of recyclable material such as a trashcan to grow cucumbers and requires no electricity or pump. A trashcan is all that is needed which is filled with water, the correct amount of fertilizer and a lid. Seeds of the cucumber plant are transplanted into a forestry tube that is then put into the lid. The system requires no additional water or nutrients, which makes it truly cheap. Usually, one batch of the crop is terminated as soon as the nutrient solution runs out.

The container should be around 30 – 35 gallons and will use a non-circulating method.

Due to the feasibility of this hydroponics technique, it is widely used in high school or college demonstrations, beginner farmers and enthusiasts. The technique is extremely valuable as it allows an individual to learn a great deal about hydroponics systems and how they work without the need for complex and expensive equipment. Weed and pesticide control can also be achieved quite easily by using a plastic weed mat and placing it below the container; the mat should preferably be black in color. Finally, the system can be transformed into a permanent trellis system that means that the container can be used over and over again and the soil beneath it can be cultivated as well!

Equipment

- Plastic trash container with a volume of 30 – 35 gallons,

- Hydroponics fertilizer,

- Growing medium, which at all costs must include 2 of the following, vermiculite, peat, coir and perlite,

- Forestry tubes of 1 ½ inch diameter and 7 – 8 inch length,

- Cucumber seeds,

- Electric drill with ¼ inch bit and a 1 ½ inch hole saw,

Procedure

Before using a plastic container or a trash can make sure that it is cleaned of any debris, fungus or parasitic infestations. If it's not, then rinse it with water 2 – 3 times but don't use bleach. If you are having difficulty in cleaning it then rinse it several times in soap. Next, place the container on a leveled and smooth surface that has exposure to plenty of sunlight but is protected from winds and other elements. Perfect locations for growing cucumbers this way is placing the can in a greenhouse or under the overhang of a house. Areas outside the house can also be used as cucumbers are quite resilient and can tolerate rain to quit an extent.

Add 10 gallons of water, e.g. tap water into the container followed by fertilizer that would normalize the pH of the water and provide a handful of nutrients.

Fertilizer

You have 2 choices when adding fertilizer to the container.

1. You can add ½ pound of Chem-Gro 10-8-22 fertilizer or a similar variant along with 2 oz. of magnesium sulfate.

2. You can add 3 oz. of Chem-Gro 10-8-22 fertilizer along with 2 oz. of magnesium sulfate and 3 oz. of calcium nitrate.

After adding one of the two fertilizers given above, stir the contents of the tank so that the fertilizer can thoroughly dissolve within the nutrient solution. As you mix the solution some of the fertilizer may start settling down at the bottom, which shouldn't worry you at all.

Now fill the can all the way to the top until it is 1 inch from overflowing and then stir the solution once again. Avoid using water that has too much salt in it and even if the tap water has too much salt in it then it will be a better option to use rain water instead. You will need to drill 6 holes of ¼ inch each in the forestry tube that will allow the roots of the plants to properly emerge from the sides of the tube. Finally fill the tube with a handful of growing medium; be sure to tap on it gently so that the roots aren't damaged.

Use the hole saw to drill a 1 ½ inch hole right in the container's lid; the hole should be 3 inches from the edge. Next, fit the tube into the lid. Making the hole too close to the center will make the length of the tube a limiting factor.

One tube will be required for every trash container that you use and the tube that you choose must fit perfectly into the container so that any insects or pests don't make their way into the can. As the system will be placed in external environments most of the time it can act as a perfect breeding ground for mosquitoes so keeping the right dimensions is very much important. The lower portion should remain in contact with the nutrient solution at all times; 1 – 3 inches would be an optimum depth.

By now the capillary action would've begun and the medium must have started to moisten, however if it remains dry then sprinkle 1 – 2 teaspoons of water into it. Use the blunt end of a pen to make a ½ inch deep hole into the growing medium and plant 1 cucumber seed. Cover it with growing medium and add 2 teaspoons of water to moisten the medium once again. The seed should start to germinate within 2 – 5 days and if it fails to do so in this time frame then you may need to plant another one. Another technique that can obtain similar results is germinating the seeds in a forestry tube with the help of a seeding branch and transplantation within 1 – 2 weeks.

Once the roots start to emerge, avoid pulling the tube from the lid as this can have serious effects on the roots. With the passage of time the plant will grow and the nutrient solution's level will decrease. Don't add more water or fertilizer to the container as this will do more harm than good. The plants will keep growing at optimum rate as long as the nutrient solution remains constant or decreasing.

You can build a 5 – 7 foot high trellis that can act as a support to the cucumber foliage and help the vine cling. The first batch of cucumbers will be ready within 50 days or so and the crop must be terminated as soon as possible after that if the nutrient solution decreases to zero or infestations go out of control.

Upon termination empty the container into some bushes and remove any root mass from the container. Wash the can thoroughly and use it once again if you want, following the same steps.

Melissa Honeydew

Chapter 13

Other Hydroponic Vegetables

Cucumbers may be one of the most popular of the hydroponic vegetables but there are plenty of others that can easily be grown using this system.

Beets

Root crops are very easy to grown hydroponically however you do need a system that uses a fair amount of medium for growing. This is to support the plant while the root system is developing and two systems that work well are the ebb and flow and Aeroponics systems.

The container that you use must be of sufficient size to support full grown beets – on average, beets get to a couple of inches in diameter although that will depend on the variety you are growing. The container must be a minimum of 4 inches in diameter by 6 inches deep as an absolute minimum.

The container can be filled up with your choice of growing media. You can use whatever you like but perlite mixed with vermiculite is one of the best and you can even add a little peat to it if you want – this isn't necessary though.

Leave about an inch of space between the top of the container and the filler from the reservoir for a bit of headroom.

Keep in mind that beets like cool weather, surviving very well in chilly temperatures but not so well in intensive heat. Keep the temperature steady at between 60 and 65° F for a successful crop. And they will need at least six to eight hours of daylight per day so use growing lights if necessary.

You can start beets from seed very easily but if you choose to start them off in soil, make surer that you rinse off any remaining soil on the roots. The soil can cause interference in the nutrient solution so put the plants, root first, into a nutrient solution that is about ¼ of the proper strength and soak them for around 30 minutes. At this stage, a solution that is any stronger can put the plants into shock.

Nutrients

You should use a nutrient solution that is specifically designed for root vegetables. Check the label of the solution for ratios – you should be looking for ne that is around 5-10-10.

Under conventional growing conditions, beets will mature sometime between 50 and 70 days but in a hydroponics system; they can mature quite a bit earlier, in some cases, as early as 35 days. One of the good things about beets is that it isn't possible to harvest them too early because the younger roots re actually much nicer and more tender to eat. However, if intend to use the beet greens, harvest before they go over 6 inches in height otherwise the taste will start to disappear.

The biggest nutrient deficiency you will suffer is a lack of iron and this is because the beets need a lot of it and, often, the solutions just don't have enough. Even when the solution has sufficient iron, it may not all be used by the plant because of lower rates of photosynthesis, down to poor lighting. Too little iron will cause impairment to the chlorophyll biosynthesis, wasting the photosynthesis effect.

Nitric oxide is needed for the development of the fine root hairs and the capillaries. This can be given in the form of nitrogen or nitrates mixed in the nutrient solution. However, you cannot just add nitrogen in any quantity because it won't make the plant synthesize it any better. You should look into using slow-release nitrogen or by adding humic acid to the solution. This will boost nutrient uptake by the plant and is a good solution for beets grown in the hydroponic system.

Garlic

Garlic is another plant that can easily be grown in hydroponics but, as with all of them, there are the right ways and the wrong ways. Garlic is very strong in odor and growing garlic in a windowsill hydroponics system could result in your house smelling very strongly of garlic. It's best to stick to growing it in an outdoor system or one that is away from the main home if possible.

If you are growing purely for personal use, don't grow too much. Start a few plants at staggered intervals – not only will this ensure a steady flow of garlic, it will also ensure that the smell is not overpowering.

A mature garlic plant can grow as tall as one and a half feet, maybe more. You will need to make sure that your lights are adjustable in height or that you use vertical ones.

While you can start garlic from seed, it is better to buy a couple of bulbs and split them into cloves. Each clove will produce a full bulb of garlic so you won't need too many to get started. When you use store bought garlic, use only good healthy ones. Split the bulbs and leave the paper casing on each clove. Plant them in a growing media mix of perlite, perlite and vermiculite or coco coir. Make sure that the pointed end faces upwards – the roots will grow from the bigger end.

Don't plant them deep, just below the surface is sufficient and make sure you cover the tip. Keep them damp but not soaking wet. Garlic plants take around 45 to 60 days to emerge and the temperature should be kept between 35 and 50° F – they prefer colder weather. Sprouts generate at around 40° F.

One of the good things about garlic is that they don't take up much horizontal space because they can be grown close together. Keep them about three to four inches apart. You can also start garlic in a glass of water by covering the bottom half of the close in water and leaving it to sprout. Once it does remove it and put it in your hydroponic system – don't leave it too long in water or it will rot.

Light and Temperature

Light is important to garlic, at least 6 hours per day as a bare minimum. Ideally, they should have between 10 and 12 hours per day. Never leave a light burning all day and night, because garlic needs a certain period of darkness.

Once it is established, garlic is extremely hardy and will tolerate temperatures as low as 30° F for a short time and small periods of up to 85° F.

Pests and Disease

Garlic rarely suffers with pest or disease problems because they are actually natural repellents against insects. The only thing they may get is fungus diseases but they are rare.

Harvest

In a soil garden, you would harvest garlic when at least half of the have browned off but the growth is much faster in hydroponics and you will see the cloves without having to dig them up, making it easier to judge when to harvest them. When you have harvested, hang them for 6 weeks to dry off. It must be in a cool shady area that is dry and well ventilated. If you intend to replant from your own stock, keep the best bulbs back.

Lettuce

Lettuce is one of the easiest plants to grow in hydroponics, along with other leafy green vegetables. They will thrive in just about any setup and require just basic care. Lettuce is one of those plants that can be harvested a bit at a time, by just taking a few of the outer leaves off at a time. When those leaves are removed, they will quickly reproduce and his is similar to the deadheading we do with some flowers and herbs.

One of the biggest drawbacks to lettuces in hydroponics is that they mature much quicker than in conventional growing. They usually grow to maturity within a couple of weeks and, if you put too many in at once, you will have way more than you can possibly eat. In fact, hydroponics lettuce will produce more edible growth per square foot than any other fruit or vegetable plant.

Lighting

Lettuce requires some light and a simple fluorescent set up will work just as well as any other. If there is not enough light, your lettuce plants may bolt which will leave with a bitter taste and inedible. On the other hand, too much light can cause algae to grow in the water, which is not a good thing.

Planting

You can use just about any growing media but the best ones are a vermiculite-perlite mix, or Rockwool cubes. It is best to start the seeds off in an inorganic material, definitely not soil. Go for Oasis cubes or Rockwool cubes, or even coco noir. When they are ready, you can put the entire plug straight into the prepared hydroponic bed and the roots will just grow straight through the material. You can start your seeds straight in the hydroponics bed as well. Seedling should be about 14-21 days old before they are transplanted into the hydroponic system though. Keep the temperatures at around 40° F before germination and, when they start to germinate, raise it to about 65° F

Nutrients

To get the best out if it, lettuce needs to be grown very rapidly and this means it will need large amounts of potassium. Do be aware that some varieties can get leaf tip burn because they are sensitive to nitrogen, especially if the levels are too high.

Lettuce loves magnesium sulfate and calcium but these don't tend to be a part of the nutrient solutions that you can buy so you will need to add these in separately. If you are growing under warm conditions, you can use a high nitrogen solution to force the lettuce to grow faster but if you are using low light levels, like in a fluorescent light setup, the levels of nitrogen and potassium must be reduced.

Potatoes – Quick Facts

- You can grow potatoes from any potato that has an eye on it

- Keep the pH range as near to 5.8 to 6.2 as you can for the best results

- Keep temperatures at between 65 and 75° F

- Potatoes require a minimum 6 hours of daylight per day but, for best results, between 10 and 12 is best

- Keep humidity levels down as potatoes are highly prone to rotting in high humidity

For best results, grow potatoes from "slips", a slice or quarter of a potato with an eye on it. Try not to use potatoes that you buy from a supermarket as they are generally treated with some kind of chemical to stop them from sprouting. Use seed potatoes from a garden center or a catalog that specializes in chemical-free and disease free potatoes.

Planting

Plant the potato slip at the bottom of the container you use and, as the plant starts to grow, add more medium to keep the slip and the potatoes covered. If the potatoes are exposed to light, they may turn green and that is down to a toxic alkaloid, called solanine, which is bitter.

The biggest problem with hydroponic potatoes is that you nearly always get loads of small tubers; rarely will you get anything that will match traditionally grown potatoes sizes. The total weight of the harvest will also likely be much less per plant than traditionally grown.

However, things have improved somewhat in terms of the media used and the best one is a blend of vermiculite, perlite and peat. This has been shown to produce a much higher yield of bigger potatoes and in weight per plant. The perlite will draw up moisture from the base and will keep the oxygen levels at a premium. Oxygen is vital for root crops, particularly at root level because it helps the plant to absorb the nutrients you feed it. The vermiculite will help the media to retain water but, if you use tap water, you must stand it for 24 hours first, exposed to the open air, to allow the chlorine to dissipate from it.

The potatoes should be planted into the perlite, around one to one and a half inches below the surface. They should be planted cut-side down with about four to six inches between plants. Keep the container covered unless you are watering it, until you start to see shoots coming through the perlite – should be about two weeks.

At this point, you will need to give the plants light while keeping the actual potatoes covered. Add in a nutrient fertilizer at least once a week – a teaspoon of 20-20-20 containing micronutrients in one gallon of water is sufficient for the young shoots but, once your plants are a foot or more taller, change to a fertilizer with a higher level of potassium in it.

pH Levels

If your potatoes are to gain the most benefit from the nutrients, the pH level should be around 6.0, although a couple of decimals in either direction won't hurt. Most of the pH problems you might come across are easily avoided if you read the nutrient solution label properly. If your pH is way out:

- To lower it, use a small quantity of distilled white vinegar

- To raise pH, you can add sodium hydroxide or potassium hydroxide into the water but only in small amounts. If you are using hydroxides, make sure your hands are dry and only handle them with god water resistant gloves on

- Test any adjustments you make on one plant before you do it to the whole crop

Keep the temperature around 65 to 75° F as potatoes like warmer conditions but allow for good ventilation so the humidity levels are not high

Peppers

The humble pepper can be grown at any time of year and in any season in the hydroponics setup. In fact, research has shown that hydroponic peppers produce much bigger yields of much bigger and a higher quality fruit, provided it is done properly. In theory, this is because the plants are getting a steady supply of food from the nutrient solution and are less prone to attack by insects and pathogens from the soil.

The best system to start with is the ebb-and-flow system, although most hydroponics systems will work well for peppers. If you are planting from seedling stage, you must ensure that there is no soil left on the root ball. You can remove this by placing them in a container of cool or room temperature water to soak the soil off. Remove as much as you can without damaging the fragile root system. Plant the seedlings a little deeper than they were in the soil pot and only put one plant in each pot.

Space and Light

Space your pepper pots around seven to nine inches apart. If you don't get the spacing right now, it isn't too much of a problem, in hydroponics, you can simply widen the space whereas in a conventional garden, it is much harder because the plants have to be dug up and disturbed.

Peppers need around 10 to 12 hour of daylight per day so place them under grow lights, with the lights about six to eight inches above the plats. This should avoid tip scorching from happening. If you place the lights any further away, the plants will not benefit from the system and growth will be stunted. As the plants grow, you need to keep adjusting the height of the lights to maintain that gap.

Peppers produce much better if they are under a high light system so ensure that they have 10 to 12 hours per day and a period of simulated night darkness, required for the optimal results. Keep the day temperature between 73 and 80° F and nit temperatures must not fall below 70° F.

Pruning

Pepper plants need to be pruned n a reasonably regular basis, when the plants reach six to eight inches. You can do this by pinching some of the stem buds back but be sure that you know the difference between a stem and a flower bud. Peppers will produce lots of flowers and, if you remove some of these, the energy in your plant will go into producing fewer but bigger fruits rather than lots of little ones.

When the plant reaches a foot tall, early season pruning can be down and should stop when the peppers are set on the plant. You will notice that peppers tend to grow in a "y" shape with lots of smaller "y's" coming off the main stems.

When the plant reaches 12 inches in height, you will easily be able to see which the strongest branches are. Cut the smaller branches back, but be very careful that you don't do any damage to the main stem. If you do, it will affect the growth of the plant and the fruit.

Nutrient Solution and pH

If you are growing lots of different plants in the same setup then you can use a general solution. If you have one that is for tomatoes or cucumbers, it will do perfectly well for peppers.

Peppers require a pH of between 5.5 and 7.0 and in hydroponics system. If the pH is too low, you can correct it by adding in potassium hydroxide or sodium hydroxide but, as I mentioned in the last section, do not handle these with wet or ungloved hands.

Carrots – **Quick Facts**

- The optimal pH for carrots is 6.0 to 6.5 although up to 7.5 will be fine

- To ensure good vigorous growth, carrots need plenty of air flow

- For seed germination, keep the temperature between 50 and 85° F

- A minimum of 6 hours daylight per day is necessary but between 12 and 16 will give the best results

- If you stagger your planting, it is possible to harvest carrots all year round.

Planting

Fill up your chosen container with a mixture of one-third vermiculite and two-thirds perlite. You can also use coco noir or sterile sand as growing media but the perlite and vermiculite mix seems to work better for root vegetables. The media needs to be at least a foot deep in the container, more if you are growing any of the larger varieties. If it isn't deep enough, the carrots will fork out and then, when they reach the bottom of the container they will begin growing sideways.

Moisten the growing media and then sprinkle the carrot seeds on top – if you are using sand make sure that it is sterile.

Cover over the seeds with a layer of media about three quarters of an inch deep and make sure that you have over seeded by about 50%. Some of the seeds just won't germinate and others will need to be removed later on because they won't be strong enough.

The growing media must be kept warm and wet while the seeds are germinating. However, don't leave them over-wet, as this will rot the seeds and the carrots out.

Keep the temperature around 85° F and you should start to see the seeds germinate within about 6 to 10 days. When the tops appear, it's time to thin out the weakest ones – you could find that about a third of your seedlings will need to be removed. Then look to see if any of the remaining ones are growing too close together – if they are, remove some more. Carrots don't like to be overcrowded and won't grow properly.

Nutrients and pH

Carrots should be sprinkled with a nutrient solution once a day at the very least – two or three times a day is best. Only use enough solution to dampen the top layer of growing media and the plants will draw most of what they need from the lower reservoir.

Sprinkle carrots lightly with a nutrient solution at least once a day, but two - three times per day is best. Sprinkle with only enough nutrient solution to ensure that the upper layer of Growth Medium gets damp. The carrot plants will draw the bulk of their nutrients from the reservoir below.

They require a hydroponics pH of about 6.0 to 6.5, although up to 7.5 is ok – not optimal though. Carrots that are maturing need a stronger nutrient solution than those that are germinating or have formed into young seedlings. One the seedlings have sprouted, add grow lights to give them between 12 and 16 hours of daylight with 8 to 12 hours of darkness for optimal results.

Harvest

This will depend entirely on the variety of carrot you are growing and the conditions they are grown under. They should be ready for harvest within two to three months.

Never use seedlings from a soil garden in your hydroponics setup as they can bring in disease and pests. Always grow directly from seed.

Chapter 14

Growing Berries with Hydroponics

There is nothing nicer than the taste of fresh berries in the summer and fall months but they can be expensive to buy in the stores. While some areas are not suitable for growing berries outdoors, there is absolutely no reason why you can't grow them hydroponically. As with every plant, there are certain requirements:

Strawberry – Quick Facts

- The best pH range for optimal results is between 5.5 and 6.0

- Strawberries thrive in low humidity

- They need good air flow

- If humidity is too high, a powdery mildew will form on the plants

- The best temperature for strawberries to fruit in is 65 to 75° F

- They need a minimum of 6 hours of light per day, preferably 12 to 16 hours

- Grown in the right conditions, you can expect a yield of around 3 lbs. of fruit from every plant

- It is possible to harvest these plants every month but the plants will have a much shorter life expectancy

When you choose a strawberry variety, don't go for the June bearers, as they will not bear fruit after the summer, being suited for just one heavy crop. For hydroponics, you want ever bearing for day neutral varieties to get the benefits of an extended season.

Growing from seed is not really an option for hydroponics growers because plants can take between two and three years to reach maturity. Instead, look for certified virus tested runners that have been cold stored. For those that don't know, the runner is an off-shot from a mature plant. Choose runners that are either in flower or have at least one bud on them. To make sure you get a steady supply of fruit all year round, plant chilled runners at staggered intervals.

Nutrient Solution

Any media that you choose to use, be it vermiculite, Rockwool, or any other, must be presoaked for about minutes in a pH balanced water. If you use dry media, it will suck all of the moisture out of the roots of your plants.

Strawberries require three main nutrients – potassium, nitrogen and phosphorus. They also need large amounts of calcium, sulfur and magnesium, in addition to the oxygen, carbon and hydrogen that they will pull in from the air and the water. Strawberries also require trace amounts of some elements to thrive:

- Copper

- Manganese

- Iron

- Cobalt

- Molybdenum

- Chlorine

- Zinc

If your strawberry plants develop browning or yellow leaves, brown spots, poorly developed berries or the plants themselves are oddly colored, they are not getting the nutrients they require. Hydroponic strawberries will produce fruit at up to

25% faster than soil-grown plants provided they are looked after properly.

Planting

Use 5-gallon containers that are of a food grade and are clean of all chemicals. If needed, drill some holes for drainage in the bottom of them. Wash it thoroughly and dry it before filling about with your pre-soaked media up to about two-thirds full. Vermiculite is the best growing medium for strawberries but they will grow in others.

Fill up another bucker with some cool water.

If your strawberry plants are coming from a soil medium, remove the plant from the container and shake it gently to remove soil from the roots. Tap off any remaining dirt with your fingers – do try not to damage the root system in the process because even the smallest and finest of roots play their part in the health and the fruit production of the plant.

Soak the whole root system of the plant in the cool water for about 10-25 minute then remove them and wash them under cool running water to remove any remaining soil.

Remove any leaves that are dry, dead or discolored before you put the plants into the new pot. To put them in the pot, hold the crown and splay the roots out evenly above the new growing medium. Add more of the media to cover over the roots but do not cover the crown, as it needs to be exposed to the air and light.

Because your strawberry plants need between 12 and 16 hours of light a day place them near a sunny window or use grow lights.

Finally, mix the nutrients according to the instructions and water your strawberry plants thoroughly. Check the water on a daily basis and add more as needed to keep the roots moist all the time.

Care

If any flower blooms show up before the plant has reached 10 to 12 inches round, remove them and do not allow them to regrow until the strawberry plant is strong enough to support the berry weight. Cut back any runners that appear because they use up the energy that the plant needs to fruit. You can discard the runner or use them to start off new plants.

Keep an eye on the temperature – if it is too hot, growth will be slowed, the plants won't flower and they may stop producing berries. If it is too cold, they just won't grow at all. Keep the temperature between 65 and 75° F. that said, strawberry plants gain benefit from being chilled over the winter so keep them in an unheated place for the cold months. If you don't get cold seasons, you can simulate the season for new plants by dipping the roots into microbial solutions, wrapping them carefully and loosely in clear plastic and placing them in the refrigerator for up to three months.

Mist your strawberry plants once a week to keep the humidity down and make sure there is plenty of air circulation.

Finally, do not pick your berries until they are fully ripe, as they will not continue to ripen after picking.

Blueberries – Quick Facts

- The ideal pH for hydroponic blueberries is between 4.5 and 5.8.

- The ideal temperature is between 72 and 76° F

- They need a minimum of 8 hours light per day but ideally between 12 and 16.

- You cannot grow blueberry plants from seed; you will need to use transplants instead.

- Humidity range should be kept between 65 and 75%

- It is possible to harvest blueberries all year round provided you stagger the growth cycle

Blueberries are one of the most distinct of the fruit crops because of their growing requirements. For starters, they will not grow in alkaline soil, needing low pH acidic soil instead. If you try to grow blueberries in the conventional way, in an alkaline soil, they simply will not grow, no matter how much you do o the soil to make it acid. It is far easier to control this with hydroponic, making them a good crop to grow.

Do not confuse soil pH with hydroponics pH – they are two completely different things. For hydroponics, you need a nutrient solution that is between 5.5 and 6.0 pH although they will still grow at anything between 5.0 and 7.5. If the solution or the growing medium you use is too acidic or too alkaline, you will lose a lot of the vital nutrients, simply because the plants will not be absorbing them.

Planting

You can hydroponic blueberries in poly bags or grow bags with a mixture of 30% Vermiculite and 70% Perlite. The perlite doesn't really retain water; instead, it pulls the water up through a transpiration pull method. The vermiculite will retain too much water, which is why you don't need so much of it. When you are growing berry plants, although the roots have to be kept moist, you don't want them water logged or too wet for too long, otherwise root rot will set in.

Use a drip system for watering, allowing any surplus nutrient solution to drain away – don't waste it though, direct into a waste receptacle of some kind. You can reuse the drained off solution for one more cycle on your plants and the dispose of it – into your outdoor compost system if you have one.

Try to plant at least two plants of the varieties that you choose for pollination purposes and stagger your planting so that you reap the rewards on a regular basis throughout the year.

Be aware that blueberry plants can take between three and five years to become established and bear a good yield of fruit. For the first year, do not expect any harvest although, by the second one, you should be able to get some berries of the plants.

Light

Because blueberries need between 12 and 16 hours of daylight every day, use HID lamps. These are High Intensity Discharge lamps and are the ones most likely to simulate sunlight. You can use fluorescent lighting but the fruit yields will not be as good. LED lighting will work as well and, while they aren't as effective as HID lamps, they are much cheaper to run. You could consider using reflective film as well to make sure you use all of the light available to you.

Never leave your plants in the light 24 hours a day, seven days a week. Most plants require a period of darkness in their daily cycle and blueberries are no exception.

Grown in the conventional way, a blueberry plant will need around 140 days of growing season. In hydroponics, you can shorten this if the conditions are right to allow for regular yields.

However, do bear in mind that the hydroponic blueberry plant must be put into a simulated winter season for at least one month out of the year.

Pruning and Dormancy

You can avert blueberry dormancy but they do need something of a cold season for the fruit to set properly. There is little to no chance that you will be able to harvest from one single plant all year round and, as such, if that is your intention you need to have several plants. Also, if you do avert dormancy, you will get a beautiful lush plant but little to no fruit.

Plants that are grown indoors will need to be pruned more regularly than outdoor plants. Pruning will give you much better yields, in both quality and quantity. Cut out any dead wood, any of the lower growth that is discolored or excessive – aim to cut away about one third of the plant every year.

In the first year of growth, remove any of the berry or flower buds as soon as you see them. This may seem counter-productive since you are growing them for their berries but, in the first year, all the energy needs to be directed into foliage, along with all the nutrients and that can't happen if they are allowed to flower and fruit.

How to Avoid Root Rot

Root rot will destroy your plants so follow these tips carefully:

- If you are transplanting your blueberries from soil, remove all of the soil from the root ball without getting the rots saturate.

- Do not let the root system dry out during the hardening off and transplanting process. All the energy that plant uses is in the roots so do as little damage as possible when you are transplanting them

- You can use root health supplements specifically for hydroponics to eradicate root rot and you can also use horticultural peroxide. The cheapest route is to use five to 7 drops of household bleach in a gallon of water twice a week. This must be done this often because the chlorine will dissipate in the water.

Raspberries – **Quick Facts**

- The optimal pH for raspberries is between 5.8 and 6.5

- The temperature should ideally be kept between 72 and 76° F

- They require at least 6 hours of light per day, preferably 10 to 12 hours

- Growing raspberries from seeds is no recommended, use transplants instead

- Keep humidity between 65 and 75%

- By staggering the growth cycles you can harvest raspberries all year round

Raspberries are a long-term plant that grows quite large. They will push about many canes and suckers that need regular pruning. This must be done when the plant is dormant and after fruiting has occurred. Raspberry canes are biennial so the cane will grow the first year and then produce fruit the following year before dying. The only exception to this is the over bearer varieties.

Be aware that all brambles and that includes raspberries, are very susceptible to root rot and, with hydroponics, that is even more likely so care must be taken to keep it away. See the section on blueberries above for tips on avoiding root rot.

Raspberries must be pollinated to produce fruit so if you grow them indoors, you will need to hand pollinate them.

Planting

As with blueberries, you can grow hydroponic raspberries in a poly bag with a mix of 30% vermiculite and 70% perlite. Again, this is because the vermiculite retains too much water while perlite retains very little and brambles do not like to be waterlogged.

In the springtime or whichever cycle in your hydroponics system relates to spring, the nutrient solution needs to be heavy in nitrogen. However, towards the end of the growing cycle, you need to add more potassium and phosphorus.

Light, Temperature and Humidity

Although raspberries thrive in full sunlight in the garden, they will grow well with less light. You do not need to use heat lamps, instead you can use cool fluorescent lights or LED ones.

Raspberries prefer cooler temperatures so keep the daytime temperature between 72 and 76° F and overnight temperatures if around 60° F. They are not fragile plants and will tolerate fluctuations in temperature, adapting quite well.

In terms of humidity, the range should be between 65 and 75%. Anything above 90% will slow down pollination and will encourage fruit molding. Levels below 65% can also slow down pollination and encourage mites.

Supporting the Plant

Some raspberry varieties are too big for hydroponic set ups but there are lo of smaller ones that work well. However, even the small ones need support in the form of a trellis to encourage healthy plants and good production.

As the plants begin to get heavy with fruit and with foliage, they will bend over and will break on occasion. As the growing season reaches its peak, you can cut off leaves and old canes to help with this, as well as setting up a good trellis system.

Chapter 15

Training & Pruning

Hydroponics does not allow the use of soil as the whole point of using hydroponics system is going soil-less which means other growing media must be used to compensate for the qualities of soil. However, other mediums aren't as firm as soil and don't provide equivalent anchorage, therefore, growers must think of ways to support their plants artificially and train them along a static structure. Support is of detrimental importance when growing tall plants like cucumber, tomatoes, etc. or those bearing heavy fruits.

One of the ways to provide support to a plant is to tie polythene string at the base of each plant by a loose knot or using a plastic clop; the sting must be tied vertically to the horizontal support to hold the plants stationary. As the plants grow, wind the main stems around the string and in case you're growing an indeterminate crop like tomatoes, place additional paper clips to prevent them from slipping down.

For plants like cucumber, the vertical string must be attached to each of the plants with a plastic clip and as they grow, the main stem must be wound loosely around the string. Attach additional plant clops to prevent the stems from slipping. Indeterminate tomatoes on the other hand must be trained to a single stem and all lateral branches must be removed as soon as they are 5 cm long. Furthermore, the lateral branches should be pruned every 3 – 4 days. Tomato plants should also be trimmed down from time to time, e.g. 2 – 2.5 meters above the main stem. As the plants grow taller, you should start removing about 4 – 5 leaves at the bottom, untie the string from the overhead support and lower the entire plant about 60 cm. This process should be carried out every 2 weeks and the strings should be strong as well as long enough to permit lowering the crop without any untoward incident.

For cucumbers, the umbrella system of pruning can be used which involves pruning at all lateral branches until the plants reach the overhead support. When this happens, remove the terminal bud and allow the 2-side branches to grow downwards. Furthermore, cucumber can produce more than 1 fruit for every node that may be thinned out to limit the production of fruit in case the shape of the plant or the fruit is affected over time.

On the other hand, bell pepper plants can be trained at 2 stems by tying the vertical strings to an overhead support and guiding the side stems to the vertical strings. Side shoots that arise from the stems must be pruned after 3 weeks so that fruiting remains limited to only 2 of the branches.

Melissa Honeydew

Chapter 16

Requirements for Hydroponics

Hydroponics is easy to use and can be developed quite easily, however, there are a few requirements and conditions that must be met be a hydroponic system to obtain a high yield. These are listed in bulleted form below so that you'll be able to recall them easily.

- The electrical conductivity of the nutrients solution must be within 1.5 – 2.5 while the pH must be within 5.8 – 6.5. Most plants support this range and give a good yield. Any pH or electrical conductivity outside of this range would result in reduced uptake of nutrients as well as damaged roots.

- It is vital that the temperature of the nutrient solution remains constant because as the temperature goes up the rate of respiration increases, which translates into a higher demand for oxygen and decreased solubility of oxygen. The requirement for hydroponics system is more critical if they are placed in greenhouses as the temperature is guaranteed to increase during the afternoons.

- There must always be plenty of dissolved oxygen in the solution so that the roots of the plants can easily absorb it. Reduced amount of oxygen will mean reduced rate of absorption that will cause the root to rot and result in a decreased yield. In a closed system, collection of used up nutrient solution will allow aeration of the tank without any external efforts.

- When using root dipping techniques, allow a nominal air gap above the nutrient solution as the yield is directly dependent on the quantity and area of roots exposed to air. The roots absorb oxygen for the plants and in an ideal case, $2/3^{rd}$ of the youngest root must be in the air while the rest should be submerged in solution.

- Don't make sudden changes in the nutrient's concentration, pH or electrical conductivity.

- During crop growth, as the concentration of ions in the solution is inversely proportional to the solution level. An increase in ion concentration isn't healthy for plants so if this happens, you must siphon out the remaining solution and prepare a fresh batch.

- There should be adequate light for the soil-less culture plants, same as you would provide a plant grown in soil.

- Pest and disease free seedlings must be used for establishing hydroponic crops. As soon as you spot an infected plant, destroy it, otherwise the infection can spread.

- If there is a nematode problem in the solid media then remove the media as well as the plants immediately. Sterilize the growing medium and if still in doubt, replace it with new one. Furthermore, ensure that the water is free of nematodes.

- Algae can also develop with the passage of time within the tubes and block the passageway used for delivering the nutrient solution. To avoid such a problem, use black color tubes and clean the system between crops with a solution of chlorine.

- Ensure adequate spacing when growing vine crops or any other plant that requires vast area.

You must also ensure adequate quantity of nutrients to maintain crops' yield, therefore to be sure that each plant is getting enough of each element, read the following symptoms and fill any void left by insufficient nutrients.

Nitrogen

Deficiency symptom – the plant won't grow and would have a yellow color, which would develop due to a lack of chlorophyll. Younger leaves will remain green for a longer period of time while the stems and lower leaf surfaces will turn purple.

Toxicity symptom – plants will be dark green in color due to excessive foliage but will have a very restricted root system. Furthermore, the flowering cycle will be retarded.

Phosphorus

Deficiency symptom – plants will have stunted growth and will be in dark green color. Deficiency symptoms will surface first in older leaves and then spread out.

Toxicity symptom – no major symptoms have yet been found however sometimes excess of phosphorus has been found to give rise to zinc & copper deficiency.

Potassium

Deficiency symptom – the leaves will start turning yellow in color and develop dark color necrotic lesions. The tips of the leaves will also start to die.

Toxicity symptom – excess potassium may lead to magnesium deficiency.

Sulfur

Deficiency symptom – younger leaves will start to turn yellow followed by the older ones.

Toxicity symptom – there will be a reduction in leaf size. The leaves will also be poorly deformed and have a burning color.

Magnesium

Deficiency symptom – the leaves will undergo interveinal chlorosis that will start at the leaf margins and progress inwards.

Toxicity symptom – no known symptom.

Calcium

Deficiency symptom – root tips will start to die and bud development will be inhibited. Younger leaves are affected before the older ones and become distorted in color.

Toxicity symptom – no consistent symptom known yet.

Iron

Deficiency symptom – the plant will suffer from interveinal chlorosis similar to the one caused by deficiency of magnesium. The younger leaves will be targeted first.

Toxicity symptom – necrotic spots may appear that can be located through application of sprays.

Chlorine

Deficiency symptom – leaves will become wilted and would soon become chlorotic & necrotic until they attain a brown color. The roots will become stunted with the passage of time.

Toxicity symptom – the leaf tips will become burned up. The leaf abscission will turn yellow in color and the size will decrease along with lower growth rate.

Manganese

Deficiency symptom – initial symptoms include interveinal chlorosis which targets younger leaves first. With the passage of time, necrotic lesions will follow suit.

Toxicity symptom – the plant may suffer from chlorosis from time to time, chlorophyll reduction and decreased growth rate.

Boron

Deficiency symptom – the symptoms will depend on the species. Usually stems and roots die. The remaining roots may become discolored and swollen. There will be discoloration among internal tissues of the leaves along with curling, brittleness and spotting.

Toxicity symptom – the leaf tip will become yellow followed by necrosis that will begin at the tip as well.

Zinc

Deficiency symptom – the plant may suffer from interveinal chlorosis. Otherwise, there will be a reduction in leaf size and internode length.

Toxicity symptom – excess amount of zinc will lead to iron chlorosis in plants.

Copper

Deficiency symptom – younger leaves will become darker and twisted with necrotic spots.

Toxicity symptom – the plant will suffer from reduced growth along with iron chlorosis and abnormal darkening of rootlets.

Molybdenum

Deficiency symptom – the plant's roots & stems will suffer from interveinal chlorosis starting from the youngest and moving on the older ones. In some cases, marginal cupping has been observed.

Toxicity symptom – tomato leaves have been observed to turn to golden yellow color.

Melissa Honeydew

Chapter 17

Troubleshooting – When things go Wrong with Hydroponics

This chapter is designed to help you overcome any problems that you may come across during your hydroponics experience. I have covered some of the common problems that might occur and, for the purposes of this, I am going to assume that the nutrient solution you are using is of good quality and suitable for the specific plant you are using it on. If you use a reputable brand of nutrient and follow the instructions properly, you should never suffer with nutrient deficiencies so I have reserved this section for other problems.

Rust Spots Appearing on the Leaves
This could be caused by any one of a number of things:

- Fungus – treat your plants with a high quality fungicide

- Insects – sap suckers, aphids, thrips, spider mite, etc. – take a close look at the leaves on the plants. Inspect the top and the underside of each one for signs of insect infestation. Sapsucker bugs take all the sugars out of the leaves and this will leave dead patches on the leaves. This can look like rusty colored spots.

- Necrosis – you may be feeding your plants on a nutrient solution that is too strong. Necrosis is something that usually happens when a plant is flowering. Make sure your EC meter is within the recommended range for the plant

- Deficiency – Look closely at the root system of the affected plants. If they have gone a brown color, deficiency is likely to be the issue. You may also see yellowing leaves. One of the biggest causes of deficiency is an incorrect nutrient pH so check that what you have is correct and do make sure that your pH meter is not faulty! Some deficiencies exhibit themselves with rust colored spots so think about changing the nutrient solution you are using if you cannot be sure of the age or the quality of the one you are using now. Other problems with nutrients can be caused by unequal mixing with two-part packs or forgetting to mix them altogether.

- Phytotoxicity – this is basically poisoning and could be a reaction to a nutrient that you are feeding it. Check that your plants do not look sick, wilting and yellowing. Clean out all the nutrient solution that is in the system and change it down to a half-strength solution. Do not use any additives at all because it could be one of these that is causing the issue.

Treatment

It won't always be easy to determine what is causing the problem because there could be more than one issue. Because of this, we tend to use a holistic approach. So, where there are signs of root disease:

- Get the existing nutrient solution out of the system and make up a new batch. Make it at around half to three quarters of the strength that you normally feed your plants. Add a good quality fungicide in to the water and the nutrient solution – do check that you are using one that is designed to tackle root disease. Make sure that your water temperature is being maintained at between 21 and 23°. After one week, dump the nutrient solution and make it up again to the same strength. This time, don't add in the fungicide. Wait another two weeks before you add in any preventatives, like friendly bacteria and, every time you dump the tank out, add in more friendly bacteria.

Where there are no signs of root disease:

- You need to make sure that your EC and your pH meters arc working properly. Check, double check and triple check.

- Get rid of the existing nutrient solution in the system and make up another batch and about half to three quarters of the usual strength. Do not put any additive in, only the nutrient. If they are not used properly or in the wrong doses, additives can stress plants out, especially in the early growth period. If you can't guarantee the age of the nutrient or the quality of it, ditch it and replace it with a reputable one. Look at the bottoms of the bottles – if there are any signs of crystals or sediment, don't use it. Before you put the new nutrient in, flush through the growing medium with water that has been correctly pH adjusted.

- Look for signs of pests. You will often see miniscule spots on the leaves, top and underside, drill holes in the leaves, a fiber on the underside that looks like a web or an actual web on the leaves.

- Give the plants a spray with a good quality fungicide, as it could be a fungal problem.

Yellowing and Dying Leaves

This will be evident from the bottom of the plant upward, especially if the plant is in the early flowering season. The normal cause of this is root disease and what is happening is that the plant is paying the price for some major deficiencies. First, you need to look at the plant root system. If they have gone a brown color, it will likely be as a result of Phytophthora, Pythium or oxygen starvation. The latter is the most likely reason and, once again, we take a holistic approach:

Treatment

- Check your water temperature – it should be below 25° C. The optimal range is 20 to 23° C

- If you have not been aerating the nutrient, you must do so when you add it in the future

- Dump the nutrients out of the tank and refill. Add in half the strength of nutrient that you would normally use at the growth or flower stage the plant is at. Add in a systemic fungicide, one that works to dampen off fungi. Do make sure that it is a reputable and good quality one and that it is right for what you need. Use this for 7 days and then dump out the tank again. Refill and add in the half strength nutrient but do not use the fungicide this time. Wait for a further 7 days before dumping the tank out again. Refill and this time use preventatives for root disease, like friendly bacteria. Make sure you follow the usage instructions carefully. In the future, use the friendly bacteria treatment on a regular basis

Please keep in mind that oxygen starvation is the primary cause of root disease. If the water you use has come from a tap, it is likely it is treated with chlorine. This means that it is highly unlikely that you will have Pythium in the water as this normally comes in via rainwater, bore water, dam water or via the soil.

Tiny White Spots on the Leaves

There are two main reasons for this. First, it could be a fungal or mildew issue. Regular spraying with a good quality fungicide will sort out this problem.

Second, it could be an issue with aphids. Aphids are extremely quick breeders if the environment is right for them and they are so small that they often look like a load of white spots on the leaves. Keep a magnifying glass to hand and use it to take a closer look at the spots. If they are aphids, give them a spray with an insect treatment that is designed for sucking insects. If your plants are at the flowering stage, an organic spray might be a better bet.

Your Plants Are Getting Too Big

This is usually because the plants have been switched down too late, from 18 hours to 12 and 12. Another reason could be that the plant is genetically not suited to being grown in an indoor environment. This is not really likely if you have done your homework and know the plant origins and whether it can or can't be grown indoors successfully. For example, plants that have long equatorial genetics are far less suitable than those that are of a short height and an early flowering variety. Make sure you know your plant genetics and turn them down to 12 and 12 at the right time. You could also try netting the plants down as this will stop them from getting too big and will also create a canopy level that is fairly even. Be aware of any situation that may cause extreme stress to a plant because strange things can happen. For example, if the heat is too excessive, especially overnight, the gibberellins can become overactive, causing the plant to grow too quickly and too much.

Leaf Tip Burning

This could be down to two things – one, you could be using a nutrient solution that is to strong or, two, you could have a buildup of alt around the plant root system. To counteract this, flush the growing medium through with water that has been pH adjusted or with a very weak nutrient solution and then cut down on the levels of nutrients that you use.

One thing that will have an effect on levels of salt is the size of the nutrient tank you are using. In a recycling system, the plants take the water and the salts up at different rates, taking more water than they do salt. The volume of water in your tank will go down quicker but the volume of salt does not, becoming stronger as the day goes on. As a rule of thumb, have a tank that is large enough to make sure that the nutrient to water volume reduces by just 10 to 20%.

Do make sure that you salt meter is working properly. If you are not sure, check it with another one that you know does work to have your supplier look at it for you.

More Severe Burning

This could be because your nutrient tank is too small. Remember what I just said – the tank should not decrease by any more than 20%.

This can also be down to a lack of maintenance. You should perhaps be keeping a better eye on your nutrient tank, making sure it is topped up daily if necessary. Also, make sure that the pH is adjusted if you do this. Where a recycling system is used, pH can fluctuate quite wildly because of the different uptake rates of the water and salt. Because more water is taken up, the solution can become too strong and this can burn your plants.

Leaf Curl Over

If the leaves on your plants are curling upwards, this could be because the pH levels are not right. It is usually a sign that the plant is suffering from a deficiency of nutrients, mostly calcium. If the pH level is not right, it can cause problems with the uptake of the nutrients and cause efficiency issues. Check that the pH is right and that your pH meter is working properly.

Leaves Turning Purple at the End of the Flowering Season

This is pretty common when a plant is coming to the end of flowering and it is normally down to a deficiency of Phosphorus. As a plant comes to the end of its life, it can struggle to take up Phosphorus and potassium, as well as other nutrients. Increase the pH to about 6.1 or 6.2 to help combat this.

One other factor that can cause this in leaves and in stems is the night temperatures being too cold compared to the day temperatures or both day and night temperatures being too low. Check on your temperatures both daytime and nighttime and adjust if necessary.

Other than that, some plants are genetically disposed to go a purple or blue color at the end of their flowering life.

Flower Rot

This is usually caused by something called Botrytis or, as t is otherwise known, Grey Mold. This is caused by fungal pathogens and control of it comes down to preventing it in the first place. If you do not stop it from happening, once it sets in, Botrytis is virtually impossible to control. It normally gets established when the plants are late in their flowering season which makes it very difficult to treat. The type of treatment you need to use is not desirable on plants at this stage because it leaves residue on the crop. In all honesty, if you spot this on your plants pull them out and dispose of them straight away as it can spread like wildfires. If you can, burn the affected plants to stop it from spreading.

In the future, make sure you take steps to prevent it. Make sure that there is sufficient air flowing around the plants and use a silica product to reduce the chances of it happening.

Leaves Wilting

Leaf wilt is often indicative of too much heat. If your planting area is too hot, especially when the plants are very young and at their most fragile, excessive heat can cause wilting of the leaves. Place a thermometer at the height of the plant, under the lights and see what the temperature is. If your thermometer is not a minimum/maximum type, check the temperature when the lights have been on for two hours and then every three hours until the lights are switched off.

Plants Yellowing and Looking Sickly

Have a look at your plant timers. If the lights are not going off when they should be and staying on too long, they can cause a lot of problems. If your timers are working right, have a look at the root system on the affected plants – if they are brown, you have root rot and this will cause the plant to suffer.

Offshoots Appearing on Flowers

If the plants are not being allowed uninterrupted sleep, or the correct amount of darkness in their cycle this can cause offshoots. When the lights go out, make sure you do not enter the room because outside light can have an effect. Check that your timers work properly and make sure that your plants are getting 12 uninterrupted hours of darkness.

Also, check that the area around the plants is not over hot as this can cause the same problems.

Room Temperature is too High

If the temperature in your room is too hot, it can cause all sorts of problems. For a start, the growing medium could be getting too warm, as could the nutrient solution. This can lead to a starvation or oxygen around the roots. Temperatures that are too high can also affect plant growth and can stress the plants out, making them highly susceptiblc to disease.

Increase airflow by adding in fans – both air in and exhaust types. You can also get cooling devices for your lamps, like shades or water jackets.

You could also consider adding a dehumidifier or air cooler in to the system. Be careful and consider this very carefully though because humidifiers can increase the humidity levels which, in turn, increase transpiration. That decreases leaf cooling so if you choose to use a humidifier, make sure you increase airflow to counteract this.

Perhaps a better option would be to use an air conditioning system but this can be cost-prohibitive.

If your water temperature is above 25° C, try to move the reservoir outside the room – only do this if it is cooler outside than it is inside. Alternatively, freeze plastic bottles full of water and put them in the reservoir –this should ring the temperature down but do not go below 20° C.

Your Plants Are Stretching

By this, I mean that there are large gaps between the internodes. There are a number of common reasons why this may happen:

- The plant is genetically disposed to have large gas in between interned and nothing you can do will stop this.

- The night period of the cycle is too hot, and this affects the hormonal activity going on in the plant

- Using certain additives at the wrong time – this can cause an increase in gibberellin activity

- Light levels are too low - if your plants are not receiving enough light, they will stretch to try to reach the light. Also, if your lighting system is a 400-watt HPS system, in the red spectrum, and it is on for 18 hours, this is too long. When you go own to 12 and 12, the plants will stretch for the first couple of weeks but will soon settle down when they get used to it.

- Plants are not getting enough nutrients, causing it to stretch. Check that you are feeding the right amounts as per the pack instructions and also check that you are feeding the right nutrients for the plant

Smaller Yields than Normal

This could be because of a number of different factors, mostly environmental. One thing that can have an effect on the final yield quantity is how old the lamp you are using. Think about when you last replaced them. Most will bring pretty bright for about 20,000 hours but, as time passes, although the lumen may still be Ok, the color spectrum will have dropped off. This means that the red spectrum, the one that affects the hormonal changes, might not be as good as it was when you bought the lamp. As a rule, lamps should be changed every 10 months or after every third crop.

White Slime on Hoses in Nutrient Tank

This is down to a buildup of bacteria around the hoses and other equipment that is in the nutrient tank. This buildup can, on occasion, be extremely pronounced but this does not have to be a problem. Much depends on exactly what type of bacteria is in the tank –if they are friendly bacteria then it really isn't a problem. If you are using hydrogen peroxide as a sterilizing agent, there should not be any bacterial build up at all, because the bacteria should not be there.

Chapter 18

How to Preserve Hydroponics Foods

Any people are interested to know if food that is grown hydroponically can be stored and, if so, how. The answer is a resounding year and there are several ways to do it. Essentially, food that is grown in a hydroponics setup is no different to what is grown in a conventional garden, with the exception that the fruits and vegetables have more flavor, may be bigger and earlier than they would normally.

There are plenty of ways that you can store an abundance of food safely and for the long term, which means it doesn't matter if you grow too much now because you will have it for later.

Freezing

Freezing is absolutely the easiest and most convenient way of storing your hydroponic foodstuffs. All you need are freezer bags and/or containers; preferably see through ones, along with some labels.

Freezing is dead easy and it keeps food fresh, even fruits. Look in any supermarket and you will see the amount of frozen fruits that are for sale so you need not worry about having too many berries left over when the crop comes in!

Bear in mind that not everything freezes very well. Cauliflower and broccoli florets do, as do beans and peas but garden greens don't. Most greens, when defrosted end up as a heap of mush on your plate. The same goes for cucumbers and tomatoes, although with the tomatoes, this is fine if they are only to be used in soups and stews. Some plants are simply too high in water content to freeze very well, although if you have the time, you can process it first and then freeze it.

Canning

This used to be a very popular way of preserving foods and still is in many areas. One of the biggest benefits of canning is that foods retain their original shape and flavor and don't turn to mush when defrosted. It isn't an easy method but the benefits can far outweigh the hard work.

Dehydration

Some places sell dehydrating units and they are becoming hugely popular now as people start to realize that foods can be dried out for preserving. The food can be kept for much longer in a dried out state and, when you want to eat it, you can rehydrate it using water. Some vegetables are better done this way than they are frozen because the dehydration removes all of the water. When you add the water back in at the rehydration stage, you get something that is pretty near to the original constituency and texture of the vegetable.

Drying

Many herbs and indeed other plants can be dried out without using a dehydrator. Drying is a much better way of preserving and is the oldest method used. For things like herbs, you should cut them, tie the stems together and hang them in a cool dry place, upside down. Using wire mesh racks and being left in the sun or put in an oven can dry out tomatoes and grapes. Slow drying is the best method but you do need to ensure that you have adequate humidity and temperature, with some air movement. You also need to ensure that your foods are spread out properly so that there is plenty of space around each one – a pile of peppers or tomatoes on the side will not dry out effectively; they are more likely to rot.

Smoking

The final method is smoking, although this will only work for certain foods. By exposing a food to smoke for a certain amount of time you are taking the moisture out of it while giving it a smoky flavor. One of the best vegetables for smoking are thin skinned peppers.

These are just some of the best methods for preserving the overflow of produce from your hydroponic garden. On the whole, any decent method will ensure that you can enjoy the fruits of your labors for many months to come.

Chapter 19

The Benefits of Hydroponic Gardening

There are a lot of people who have begun to prefer gardening using hydroponics to the traditional methods of gardening. The only issue with this type of gardening is that the food may or may not be safe since your plants may be affected by different types of pests. You have been told a little later in the book about how you can deal with the pest situation if you ever chance up on it.

People have started to become conscious about the food they eat and have drifted towards eating organic food. But, not all-organic food is good for you since you do not know how the food has been created. There are people who stop producing organic food once they have been given the right to produce organic food. The manufacturers and distributors of organic food ten to stop worrying about the methods they use to produce the organic food and focus more on the returns that they obtain. You will find that there are a lot of foods in the market that have been called organic but are not organic at all. You will need to identify these differences before you purchase these foods.

When you use hydroponics, you will find that it is impossible for a person to cheat. You are not allowed to use any chemical in the system since that will affect the growth of the plants. If you use any pesticides or fertilizers in your system, you will find that your plants have started to wither. You have to ensure that you do not have even one milligram of such a harmful chemical in the system. Since you are not allowed to use chemicals, even the ones that have been made organically, you will find that the hydroponics system is the safest way to produce organic food!

The fact that you will need to stash in your mind is that the hydroponics system does not need any chemical in order to function. It helps in producing a harmonious effect between all the elements of nature naturally. The nutrients that the fertilizers provide your plants with are already found in the nutrient solution. You will find that your plants grow tremendously well!

Other Benefits

Farming
The best benefit of all the other benefits obtained is that you obtain the knowledge of better techniques for farming. You will find that you have a yield that is either twice or even thrice the

yield you would obtain if you used traditional methods of farming. There are times when you will be able to obtain a yield that is four times the yield obtained from conventional farming!

When you use all the land you own for tradition, you will be wasting a lot of water. Most of the water you use will go into cleansing the soil and will generally seep into the bedrock. It is a very little amount of water that is absorbed by the roots of the plants. You may wonder how I am saying this when in reality hydroponics uses a lot of water too! But, the reality is that the water is always being circulated which ensures that there is no water that is being wasted.

You will also find that you do not have to pull the weeds out since the plants grow in a medium that is controlled well. You will find that the plants have grown twice as fast as they would in traditional farming. This is because of the nutrient solution that contains all the minerals and vitamins your plants need. This also means you do not have to work twice as hard or even spend too much money! All you need to do is get the proportions right!

Environment
When you use fertilizers and pesticides, the chemicals in both will begin to seep into the soil and will ten to pollute the ground water. This would pollute the other water bodies that are

connected to the ground water through the runoffs. When you use hydroponics, you will find that you do not have the need to use any extra fertilizer or pesticide to keep your plants healthy. They are extremely healthy and give you a great yield! This is because of the fact that there is enough supply of food.

You will also be able to conserve a lot of land through the hydroponics system. You will find that you use extremely small amounts of space to set up the system when compared to traditional methods of farming.

Health

The organic fertilizers are usually obtained from animals thereby causing a risk to the plants. These fertilizers may have certain pathogens that would cause the plants to become harmful or even transmit the diseases to the human beings and other living beings.

Chapter 20

How Will You Groom the Plants?

Most people are always worried when they realize that they have to start grooming their plants. You have to groom your plants since you need to ensure that the plants are not infested by pests. There are four ways by which you can groom these plants. You may be worried about how you will use these techniques to groom your delicate plants. Yes, it is true that the plants you grow in the system are delicate. But, this does not mean that you let the plants be attacked by pests. There are times when you may make mistakes as well. But, that is all right. It has rightly been said that failure is the stepping-stone to success. If you forge ahead, you will be able to make sure that you get the grooming aspect correct!

Pinching

You will need to use your thumb and your finger to hold onto the part of the stem you want to cut. This is called pinching. You will be able to keep the plants neat and compact while ensuring that you retain the shape of the plant. You have to remember to always pinch above a node since you do not want to hurt the plant in any way. It is always good to use this method of grooming if you are grooming a soft-stemmed plant. If you are unable to pinch the plant, use a pruner.

Pruning

You have to first ensure that you have sharp prune shears before you begin to trim the plants that have stems that are woody. You have to remove every part of the plant that may be injured even slightly. You will have to do this soon in order to ensure that you do not allow diseases to form. Make sure you always prune your plants during spring since they end up growing extremely fast!

Deadheading Flowers

You have to remove any dryer dead leaf or flower. This is because you have to avoid the growth of a grey mold, which would spread numerous diseases.

Cleaning

You have to always keep the system clean. Only when the leaves and flowers are without any dust will they begin to attract all the sunlight they need in order to keep them healthy. Make sure that you clean the leaves using a damp cloth while you clean rough leaves using a brush.

Handy tips and tricks to remember

When you begin to work on a hydroponics system, you will find that there are a few things that will help you throughout the journey. There are times when you may be overwhelmed when you go over the multiple things you will need to keep in mind when you are working on the system. You will start worrying which will make things worse. Just follow the process and you will be just fine.

1. Make sure that you wash every piece of equipment you will be using before you put it into the system. You have to ensure that you do not have anything dirty in the system otherwise you will be creating a huge situation for you to deal with.

2. When you are looking at the different types of medium in which you want to grow your plants, you have to understand their pH before anything else. You need to make sure that the pH will not cause any fluctuations in the system.

3. When you send your water samples out for testing, you may find that the water contains chlorine. You can use Vitamin C to remove all the excess chlorine from the water.

4. You have to ensure that for the nutrient solution, you use the right amounts of the minerals and vitamins. You have to make sure that you do not overdose your plants with nutrients and minerals.

5. You have to ensure that you use products that are eco – friendly. Make sure that every product you use has either minimal or no chemicals in it. The chemicals only find ways to bring your system down.

6. There are possibilities that there are pests on your plants. You will need to get rid of them as soon as possible. Make sure that you create a solution with vinegar and water, which you can spray on the plants to get rid of the pests.

7. If the plants are out in the open, you have to ensure that they are covered well. They should be kept away from any harm that might come to them on being placed outside!

Chapter 21

Advantages and Disadvantages of Hydroponic Gardening.

It is important to look into all aspects of something before you start with it. This applies for hydroponic gardening as well. Getting a brief yet clear look at the advantages as well as disadvantages of this system will help you get a better understanding. You can then easily decide if it is something that would be beneficial or feasible for you.

Advantages:
Environmental benefits are probably the key advantage that the hydroponic system has over others. Including this there are quite a few points to be noted.

- The amount of fertilizer used is less than half of what is normally required. This is because the growing solution is circulated and absorbed by the plants without any settling occurring. No crystallization is seen in the soil either.
- The amount of land required to grow the crops is also lesser. In normal gardening you would need

nearly double the amount of space for the same number of crops to be produced. This allows a lot of land to be preserved for other purposes instead of being used for agriculture.

- The harvesting process is also fairly simple in hydroponic gardening. The amount of labor required is reduced as well.

- Toxic pesticides also do not need to be sued since soil is not a factor here. Thus there are no pests as such that need the large amount of pesticides that are usually used. This is much better for the environment as well as for producing healthier food.

- The amount of water that normal gardening uses is ten fold the amount that is used for hydroponic gardening. It makes a huge difference in places with water scarcity or those dependent on irrigation systems. This has a huge environmental impact in a positive manner. Much more water is conserved and this is important in the current state of global warming.

- Soil in different places is different and may or may not be suitable for agriculture. With the aid of hydroponics, just about any food can be produced locally since soil is not a factor anymore. This is significant in reducing the consumption of fossil fuels for transporting food from one place to another.

- The acid and base balance can also be maintained easily.

- The need to weed, till or even mulch the soil is eliminated in hydroponic system. This helps the farmers to a great extent.
- Hydroponics can also yield multiple yields in a year since it is not dependent on seasonal changes if artificial lighting is used. This will increase the food produce to meet the growing population throughout the world.

As you can see, there are so many advantages that might convince to try out hydroponic gardening. Especially, considering the environmental benefits.

Disadvantages:

- The initial cost of setup or the investment factor is something that needs to be looked into. All the equipment that is required to set up the system is the initial cost. After that, the expenditure is minimal.
- The gardening can be affected by problems related to power supply. For instance, it can be a problem in power outages or if the pumps fail.
- Water borne diseases or organisms can affect the entire yield fast as it spreads quite quickly.
- Trial and error plays a big role. There is no exact formula for successful gardening using hydroponics. You just have to figure it out.
- Constant supervision is required for this system to work and bear fruit.
- Technical expertise is a must for managing hydroponic gardening.

- The production is limited compared to the normal type of gardening.

Keep both the advantages as well as the disadvantages in mind before investing or delving your hand into hydroponics. Only if you can manage to overcome the disadvantages is it possible for you to take advantage of the benefits of this system.

Chapter 22

Hydroponics Dos and Don'ts

Dos
Maximize the light

Light is extremely important for your hydroponic plants. Just because they are growing out of a pipe system does not mean they do not need the requisite light. You have to ensure that fruit and vegetable plants get enough and more light to prepare their food. You can look up how much light the particular plant needs and subject them to the same.

Look at the carbon dioxide content

As you know, most plants require carbon dioxide in abundance. You have to check if the plants you have need an extra dose to grow properly. You will have to look up the requirements of the plants first and then decide on adding some extra. However, remember to do everything in limit. You must not add in too much of something as that can ruin your plants. You can also seek sound advice from someone who is experienced.

Best area

Enough emphasis has been laid on the importance of finding the best area to grow your hydroponic plants. When it comes to hydroponics, you have to look for a place that receives that right amount of light; the water can flow properly and also have enough air circulation. It is only possible for you to find the appropriate place if you do regular rounds of the garden and find the best place that there is. Once you find it, you can set up the hydroponics system. A little amount of trial and error will go a long way in helping you find the best area to grow your plants.

PH levels

When it comes to hydroponics, you have to care for the medium to a large extent. It is not the same as plants growing in earth soil and you should take care of what they are being exposed to. You have to check the PH level to see if it is ideal or whether you have to add in something to balance it out. You can make use of solutions that are available in stores and use them to add to the mix and enrich it. Remember that you can both reduce and increase the PH level and must know what needs to be done.

Pump quality

It is important to make use of a great pump to help your plants grow well. The pump is what carries the water containing the nutrients and your hydroponics system will work only if you make use of a good system. You have to buy the pump system from someone reputed. You will also have to do some research in advance to ensure that you are buying something that is well reputed.

These form the various dos that you must undertake when you wish to start hydroponic gardens.

Don'ts
Don't let pests take over

When you set up an artificial system, it will surely attract a lot of unwanted attention from pests. The plants you grow will be removed from their natural setting and you will have to be really careful. You will have to inspect the area from time to time and ensure that pests have not gotten the best of your garden. You should make use of natural deterrents and avoid chemicals as much as possible. You can also grow plants that repel the insects and ensure that your garden is always protected.

Don't have bad lighting

It is extremely important for you to appropriate lighting when you wish to grow plants through hydroponics. The light should be natural as much as possible so that your plants can grow well in a natural setting. You can also make use of artificial lights if you want but must ensure that it is reaching the designated area abundantly. Bad lighting is a cause for many hydroponics systems failing and you surely don't want to encourage that in your garden.

Don't ignore temperature

Since the plants in the system will be exposed to a lot of water, it will be important for you to maintain the ideal temperature at all times. That is only possible if you place the system in a warm spot. If your plants need a moist or cold temperature then you must artificially simulate that as well. As long as your plants are happy in the temperature setting that you are providing to them, your hydroponics garden will thrive. Remember that the tops part of your plants will need a warm temperature while the root level will need to be cool.

Don't ignore weeds

It is extremely important to ensure that weeds are not growing in the system. These weeds will unnecessarily eat into your plant's nutrition. You have to try and get rid of them by inspecting the garden on a regular basis. Initially, there will be a spurt of weeds in your garden but with time, you will see that they have gradually reduced owing to you pulling them out and not allowing them to disperse their seeds. Growing strong plants will ensure that the weeds are all controlled and that the plants you have planted are thriving.

Don't forget to trim

It is important for you to trim your hydroponics garden from time to time to ensure that all the plants have their own space and are not eating away into each other's. It is a known fact that plants grow at an elevated pace in the hydroponics system and so, you must keep an eye on it. It is best for you to have a specific time frame within which you must trim the plants. That way, you know exactly when to prune your plants.

Don't forgo health checks

It is important for you to ensure that the plants you are growing are all in good shape. Check for their health from time to time and that any diseases are at bay. We looked in detail at the different types of diseases that can affect your plants and what you should do to control them.

These form the different don'ts that you should observe in order to grow the best plants.

Melissa Honeydew

Chapter 23

Myths About Hydroponics

Myth Hydroponics is a recent technology

Fact Hydroponics has existed for a long time. Right from the Egyptians to the Babylonians, people depended on hydroponics for their produce. Although most preferred to use soil as the growing medium, the invention of hydroponics brought in a new revolution. There was no need to rely on potting mixes and all that people had to do was transplant the plants into nutrient rich water. The famous hanging gardens of Babylon are said to have been hydroponic gardens.

Myth Hydroponics is unnatural and plants will suffer

Fact This is another big myth that needs to be busted. Many people assume that hydroponics causes plants to grow unnaturally and a certain amount of genetic mutation occurs. However, this is not true. The hydroponics system helps plants grow in a natural environment. There is nothing unnatural about it. The system will provide the plants with the nutrition on a timely basis. Since all of it is mostly automated, you don't have to do anything towards it. Your plants will produce organic produce when you grow them through hydroponics.

Myth Hydroponics is harmful towards the environment

Fact No. this is just a myth. In fact, it is just the opposite. The hydroponics system is much more eco-friendly as compared to regular farms. Fewer pollutants are released into the atmosphere and more importantly, almost 90% less water is consumed thereby conserving natural reservoirs. The system also prevents unnecessary run offs into natural water bodies. So you don't have to worry about any excess water from your gardens escaping into the natural environment. So you will be doing the environment a big favor by switching over to the hydroponics system.

Myth Hydroponics is quite complex

Fact Hydroponics is fairly simple. There is nothing too tough to understand and is definitely not rocket science. Once you get the hang of it, you will know how to go about growing the plants and trees. It will get progressively easier for you and you will know to control the temperature, add in the nutrients etc. It might take you a year or so to establish your hydroponics garden and from then on, it will be an easy ride. There is a lot of scope for hydroponics and will help you establish a set farming system.

Myth Hydroponics is slightly expensive

Fact Not at all! Hydroponics is not expensive at all! In fact, it will work out to be a bit cheaper than regular gardens. You need not buy as much equipment and will also not have to take too much care about the plants. You must look at it as a one-time investment. Once the system is set up, you can indulge in crop rotation. You can remove the existing crops and then sow new ones. You can also maintain a budget to know how much is being spent and whether you are making the right investments.

Myth My country will not support it

Fact This is just a myth. Your country has nothing to do with the system. Many countries all over the world indulge in the art of hydroponics. So don't worry about yours not supporting it. Once you find a dealer, you can avail help in setting it up. Once it is set up, you can carry out your gardening on a regular basis. A lot of information is present on the internet and will surely help you set up your hydroponic system.

Myth The system only works outdoors

Fact No, the hydroponics system will work indoors as well, provided you control the temperature. Under the sun, it is easier for your plants to grow as they will be exposed to a natural setting. On the other hand, setting it up indoors will mean controlling it by yourself. So, you have to know as to how to regulate the temperature, automate the water, add in the nutrients etc. Not having proper knowledge of these aspects will prevent your indoor garden from thriving. So, you have to read up on the requirements and ensure that you know what needs to be done in order to set up an internal hydroponic garden system.

Myth Hydroponic gardens don't invite pests

Fact No, this is a myth. If there is a garden then there will surely be pests. It is difficult to separate the two. You will have some uninvited guests in your hydroponics garden and you have to prepare to combat them. You have to remain as proactive as possible and ensure that the garden is well protected at all times. If at any time you do spot an infestation then you will have to deal with it with immediate effect. You have to make use of a natural pesticide to deal with these pests and keep away from the harsh chemical laden pesticides.

Myth Hydroponics can be illegal

Fact Not really! As was mentioned earlier, there is nothing wrong in growing plants through the hydroponics system. But if there are strict rules in your country then it is best that you find out about them first before undertaking this type of gardening. If you plan on growing plants that are illegal to grow in your country then you will be jeopardizing your gardening hobby. So it is best for you to know what is legal to grow in your country and what is not and only then invest in them.

These form the different myths on the topic of hydroponics.

Melissa Honeydew

Chapter 24

Bonus- Flower hydroponics

As you know, it is wise for you to grow your own fruits and vegetables in your garden in order to remain self-sufficient. However, you need not limit yourself to just these and can diversify as much as possible.

It need not always be related to food alone and you can also grow flowering plants to remain satisfied with your garden.

In this bonus chapter, we will look at ways in which you can grow flowers in your hydroponics garden.

Although most flowering plants will need a nutrient rich soil mix to grow well, you can also grow some in the hydroponics system by making use of the right techniques.

Lavender

Lavenders are great to grow in your hydroponics garden. They will add in a touch of freshness and improve how your garden looks. You will see that your garden smells fantastic all year round thanks to your lavender garden. Start by preparing the system for the plants. You have to ensure that they are spaced at distance of at least 18 inches. That is when they will grow best. The PH level should lie between 6.1 and 8.5. It will take around a month for the plants to germinate and start growing. They will require full sun and will also need a decent amount of heat to grow properly.

Chrysanthemum

Chrysanthemums are great to grow in hydroponic systems. They are amazing for most flowering plants and will help grow big and bright flowers. Chrysanthemums prefer a PH level between 4.5 and 8.5. They will need full sun and you must also provide them with adequate heat in order for them to thrive. You can choose from a lot of colors and all of them will look equally nice in your garden. It is best for you to place them close to lavenders.

Roses

Roses also do well in a hydroponics system. Roses can be a little high maintenance but they are worth the effort. Planting roses in your garden will almost always help you have a constant bloom. There are many varieties to choose from ranging from regular ones to button roses. All varieties are easy to grow and maintain. You have to use the NFT system to grow the roses.

Once you get the saplings, you have to immerse them root down in water to remove any excess soil and then plant them in the system. It will take only a short time for them to bloom. You have to remove dried and dead flowers and plant tips from time to time to ensure that your plants thrive.

Petunias

Petunias are fairly simple to grow and you don't have to do too much for it. You can buy their tiny seeds and grow them in your hydroponic garden. The seeds can be a bit expensive and so, you have to do your best to get as many to germinate as possible. Petunias, like roses, come in various colors and you can choose the ones that suit your garden. It is important for you to start them in a nursery and then transplant them once they reach a sizeable height. Your petunias will need 5 hours of full sun and some amount of heat to thrive.

Marigolds

Marigolds are a lot like chrysanthemums. They will grow well in bright spots and produce beautiful flowers. Marigolds are started from their seeds which are present inside the corolla of the flower. You can buy a few flowers, cut them open, remove these seeds and dry them before starting them in the nursery. You can then transplant them in the hydroponics system. It generally takes a month for them to germinate and before you can transplant them. Marigolds come in various colors including hybrid ones.

Daisies

It is a must for every gardener to have daisies in their garden. Daisies are beautiful white flowers that bloom all year long if the right temperatures are maintained. Daisies prefer well-draining soil and so, you have to ensure that they are not always immersed in water. They will start rotting if their roots are dipped in water all day. You might have to use bark pieces, perlite and moss to help them stay put in the system. Daisies can be low maintenance but you will have to dead head them from time to time of you wish to have them produce bright blooms for a long time.

Zinnias

Zinnias are colorful flowers that will increase your garden's aesthetic appeal. There are a lot of different varieties to choose from and each one will enhance your garden's look. In fact, you don't even have to plant them separately as all of them can go into the same system. You can buy their seeds and start them in a nursery or can also but small saplings and transplant them. They will grow fairly fast if they are exposed to the right atmosphere. Once the flowers appear, they will remain in bloom for a very long time. A new layer of petals will start to appear below the existing flower thereby increasing its shelf life.

Peace lily

If you are looking to grow an indoor plant in your hydroponics then peace lily is the one for you. Peace lilies are indoor plants that produce white flowers. They are easy to grow once you transplant them. The flowers they produce are actually modifications of their leaves and so, will not require too much sun to bloom. They will thrive in wet conditions as do most lilies.

Spider plant

If you are looking to increase the green in your garden and don't really want too many flowers then you can pick the spider plant. This plant produces long spindly leaves that droop down making the plant look like a spider. They love water and will thrive in your hydroponic system. Spider plants generally last very long and are easy to maintain. But they attract a lot of insects so you have to keep an eye on them.

These form the different flowering plants that you can grow in your hydroponics system.

Melissa Honeydew

Chapter 25

Pests to Expect and Deal With

Bad insects

Aphids

Aphids are small lice like insects that love to nest on your plants. They prefer to settle on the under surface of the plant and eat away into the nutrition. Aphids multiply rapidly and tend to leave behind small black spots. Not all aphids are black and can also be green yellow or white. Each variety is just as dangerous as the other and will surely affect your hydroponics garden in a negative way. If you don't control the first few aphids in your garden, you will have thousands in no time.

Spiders Mites

Mites or spider mites are related to spiders and have long spindly legs. They are capable of sucking out all the nutrition and life from your plants. Spider mites are mostly interested in sucking the sap that lies inside the leaves. Just like ticks, they will be waiting with their legs stretched out and stick to anything that is moving past them. They will then deposit themselves on the plants and start sucking out the nutrition. Allowing spider mites to remain on plants will mean allowing them to destroy the plants.

Mealy bugs

Mealy bugs are just as common in gardens as aphids. They multiply rapidly and leave behind a lot of eggs that hatch into newer ones and the cycle keeps going. It is believed that a single female can lay about 100 eggs every minute and that simply translates to a lot of mealy bugs. You have to get rid of them as soon as you see them to ensure that your plants are safe from a mealy bug infestation.

Miners

Miners or leaf miners are tiny insects that enter the middle surface of the leaf and start consuming the nutrition that is present there. Once they remove the nutrition, it leaves behind lines and rows of gaps that make it look like worms. These miners move like snakes there by creating a zigzag pattern. Leaf miners are comparatively easy to deal with and you don't have to do too much for them. Simply removing the particular leaves and discarding them will help you get rid of them. If a lot of the leaves have been affected by them, then it is best for you to remove and discard them in batches. Getting rid of too many at once might affect the plants negatively.

Thrips

Thrips are possibly the worst insects in your garden as they can eat away all the pollen that your plants produce. If there is not enough pollen then your plants will not be able to reproduce. That can be a bad thing. You have to control the Thrips as much as possible to ensure that your garden is blooming.

Leaf hoppers

Leaf hoppers are tiny insects that hop around and consume whatever they can find in the garden. They are particularly bad for fruits and vegetable gardens as that is their main diet. They can single handedly destroy an entire garden full of fruits, which is a bad thing.

Good insects

You must encourage some good insects to live in your garden so that you can protect it and keep it safe from bad ones. Here are some of the best insects to encourage in your garden.

Lacewing larvae

The lacewing larvae are great for your garden as they will effectively eat other bad ones. They will prey on soft bodied insects and eat them away. These lacewing larvae can look sinister but it is important that you identify them and not kill them. They have sharp pincers in front of their mouth which they use to pierce the insects.

Ladybirds

Ladybirds are every gardener's best friends. They tend to establish colonies and consume other insects. This makes sure that you have no bad insects growing in number in your garden. Lady birds are generally red in color with tiny black spots on their wings but can also be green in color. Some gardeners buy them in bulk and allow them to stay in their gardens.

Praying mantis

Praying mantises are great for your garden as they will hunt down other insects. They have a voracious appetite and will almost always hunt down other small insects in your garden. They usually arrive in pairs and you must encourage them to remain in your garden.

Earthworms

Many gardeners wonder if it is possible for them to introduce vermicomposting to hydroponics. The answer is yes. You can very much make use of worms in your hydroponics garden if you wish to enhance its output. As you know, worms tend to increase the growing capacity of plants and will do the same for your hydroponics garden. It is said that red worms and hydroponics are a match made in heaven and will help your plants grow well. You can ask for help in your local garden to set up the vermicomposting system.

Apart from these remedies, you can also make use of neem. Neem is a plant that is extensively grown in India and its leaves have a lot of medicinal properties.

Neem is extremely effective in getting rid of insects as they cannot tolerate its pungent flavor. All you have to do is find some good quality neem oil, mix it in adequate water and then spray it on the leaves. This will effectively get rid of all the unwanted insects. You can also grind up a few leaves and add it to water before spraying it on the plants.

Adding in a little clove oil as well will further enhance the insect fighting capacity of the mixture.

But make sure you only spray a little on the plants as too much can destroy your plants. You have to thin it down as much as possible and spray from a distance. You can spray a little more on the areas that are affected by the insects.

Melissa Honeydew

Key highlights

The very first thing to understand is the meaning of hydroponics. As you know, all plants and trees require soil to grow efficiently. But it is also possible for you to grow them in water alone. Better known as a hydroponics system, you are required to sow the plants in water where they will thrive and bloom. Essentially, it is a soil less system where nutrient rich water is used to nourish the plants.

The nutrients that are supplied to these plants include nitrogen, phosphorous and potassium which are essential for plant growth. Apart from these there are also some other nutrients such as calcium, magnesium and iron that are added in to enhance the growing medium.

In this day and age where inflation is rife, it becomes all the more important for people to turn self -sufficient. One great way of doing so is by making use of a hydroponics system. You can grow fruits, vegetables and herbs in your own home and not have to travel to the market for anything. You can choose from a large variety of produce and have a consistent supply all year long.

There are many varieties of hydroponics systems and you can pick the one that suits your needs the best. Most will produce similar results and so, you don't have to worry about having picked the wrong type. However, a little initial research will go a long way in helping you zero in on the best system to pick. We looked at 4 of the best hydroponics system that you can choose from and you can go through it again if you wish to understand them better. Each one comes with its own set of advantages and disadvantages and you must pick the one after understanding them thoroughly.

You have to pick the fruits and vegetables depending on the season as that will ensure a constant supply. You can make a list of the ones you wish to grow and then plant them according to their season.

As you know, it will be quite a change for your plants to grow out of a water system and so, you have to train it to grow efficiently. You will have to pick the right settings, temperature, sunny spot etc. You will also have to train it to climb up walls and trellises. It is important for you to maintain your hydroponics garden and get rid of any dried and dead materials.

It is extremely important for you to control the growth of weed in your garden. Weeds can crop up pretty much anywhere and will eat away into your plant's nutrition. You have to check your garden from time to time to make sure that there are no weeds growing anywhere. You will see a big spurt initially but will be well under your control after a while. You can look up the most common types of weeds that grow in gardens and deal with them individually.

If you wish to have a constant supply of the vegetables and fruits then you must preserve them. There are many preservation techniques to pick from like freezing, dehydrating and canning. You can preserve them for up to a year by picking the right technique.

You have to be aware of the pests that can enter your garden and affect your crops. These pests can be quite pesky and ruin your entire garden if you don't rout them out at the earliest. It is best for you to check your garden every day so as to prevent any infestations from growing in size.

We looked at the most common dos and don'ts of hydroponics that you have to follow in order to have your garden thrive. You can go through them again if you wish to understand them better.

We busted some of the common myths on the topic to help you separate fact from fiction. They will push you in the right direction.

Apart from fruits and vegetables, you can also grow pretty flowers in your hydroponic garden. We looked in detail at some of the best ones that you can grow and following the instructions will help you have a constant supply of fresh flowers all year long. You can also consider packing and selling them and establish a parallel source of income.

Patience is a virtue when it comes to gardening and the same extends to your hydroponic garden. You have to remain patient with it and ensure that you are doing the right thing at the right time. Remember that it should go beyond a hobby and you must take up hydroponic gardening as a lifestyle choice.

Conclusion

Thank you again for purchasing this book!

I hope this book was able to help you learn the basic techniques of hydroponic gardening. From here, you can enhance your skills by reading about advanced hydroponic systems but if you are doing it as a hobbyist then experimenting with the current units will be enough to grow plants in this way.

There really is very little that you cannot grow in a hydroponics setup. Most fruits, vegetables and herbs will thrive in the system, provided you use the correct nutrients for the types of plants you are growing. One thing I will say is that you cannot just set up a hydroponics system and leave it to its own devices, expecting to find a flourishing crop.

In a garden, the plants take a lot of nutrients out of the air and the soil, although this is also where many of the diseases come from. In the hydroponics system, you have to give the plants their nutrients and failure to do so will mean certain death for your plants. You have to maintain the temperatures and the humidity levels, both in the air and in the water tanks.

You must inspect your plants on a regular basis to make sure they are not suffering.

To start with, it will take a lot of learning and a lot of experimenting to get it right, especially with the nutrient side of things. You also need to ensure that you give your plants a proper day and night cycle; there are very few plants that can survive without a period of darkness – this is when the plants rest and recuperate, the same as a human being does and you must make sure that your plants get the rest they need, preferably undisturbed.

Finally, once you get it right, you can enjoy a bountiful harvest, with many times the flavor and taste than conventionally grown vegetables and fruits. You can also enjoy longer harvesting seasons if you learn how to stagger the plantings successfully.

Hydroponics may be hard work to start with but the rewards really are worth the hard work. And, you can rest safe in the knowledge that, when it all comes together, when you reap a wonderful harvest, you know it was all down to you, all down to the hard work and careful monitoring that you put in, careful measurements of nutrients and preventing disease and insect problems.

Thank you for Reading! I Need Your Help...

Dear Reader,

I Hope you Enjoyed "**Hydroponics for Beginners: The Ultimate Guide to Hydroponic Gardening**". I have to tell you, as an Author, I love feedback! I am always seeking ways to improve my current books and make the next ones better. It's readers like you who have the biggest impact on a book's success and development! So, tell me what you liked, what you loved, and even what you hated. I would love to hear from you, and I would like to ask you a favor, if you are so inclined, would you please share a minute to review my book. Loved it, Hated it - I'd just enjoy your feedback.

As you May have gleaned from my books, reviews can be tough to come by these days and You the reader have the power make or break the success of a book. If you'd be so kind to CLICK HERE to review the book, I would greatly appreciate it!

Thank you so much again for reading "**Hydroponics for Beginners: The Ultimate Guide to Hydroponic Gardening**" and for spending time with me! I will see you in the next one!

Free Bonus!!!

We would like to Offer you Exclusive access to our Breakthrough Book Club!!! It's a place where

We offer a NEW FREE E-book every week! Also our members are actively discussing, reviewing, and sharing their thoughts on the Book of The Week and on topics to help each other Breakthrough Life's Obstacles! With a Chance to win a $25 Gift Card EVERY Month! Please Enjoy Your FREE Access to the **Breakthrough Book Club**

Check Out More From The Publisher...

Marriage: Romance Your Mate Again, With Spicy Sex Secrets, Pleasure, Taboo And Sex Positions that will Blow Their Mind

by Veronica Counsel

http://www.amazon.com/Marriage-Pleasure-Positions-Intimacy-Counseling-ebook/dp/B016SGTEY2

Paleo: The Ultimate Paleo Mass Gain Plan: How to Add Muscle and Gain Weight on the Paleo Diet

by John Grokowski

http://www.amazon.com/Paleo-Workout-Supplement-Building-Crossfit-ebook/dp/B01573FAIG

Psychology: Hypnosis & Mind Control – To Overcome Stress, Anxiety, Depression & Finally Recover Your Happiness

by Fred McGaughy

http://www.amazon.com/Psychology-Hypnosis-Depression-Happiness-Brainwashing-ebook/dp/B014AMVA3E

Healthy Living: Mental Health, Find Happiness by Improving your Gut Health, Sugar Addiction, and IBS

by Maria Lexington

Melissa Honeydew

http://www.amazon.com/Healthy-Living-Happiness-Schizophrenia-Fibromyalgia-ebook/dp/B010KM9CLA

Survival: The Survival Guide for Preppers, Make Yourself Ready Through Hunting, Fishing, Canning, and Foraging

by Jack Campbell

http://www.amazon.com/Survival-Preppers-Permaculture-Bushcraft-Hydroponics-ebook/dp/B01573FBP8